Western Civilizations

Brief Edition

VOLUME 2

STUDY GUIDE

Western Civilizations

Volume 2

BRIEF EDITION

Margaret Minor

NICHOLLS STATE UNIVERSITY

Paul Wilson

NICHOLLS STATE UNIVERSITY

 W • W • NORTON & COMPANY • NEW YORK • LONDON

ISBN 0-393-92586-2 (pbk)

W. W. Norton & Company, Inc., 500 Fifth Avenue, New York, N. Y. 10110
        www.wwnorton.com
W. W. Norton & Company Ltd., Castle House, 75/76 Wells Street, London W1T 3QT

1 2 3 4 5 6 7 8 9 0

CONTENTS

PREFACE

This *Study Guide* is designed to complement *Western Civilizations*, Brief Edition, by Coffin and Stacey. It is specifically addressed to students as a user-friendly manual that will enable them to grasp the significance of the material covered in each chapter. Instructors will find it beneficial to assign the *Study Guide* to improve student comprehension and to use certain parts of it for tests, quizzes, class discussions, and research assignments. The *Study Guide* provides a step-by-step approach to each chapter in *Western Civilizations*. We have designed exercises to promote understanding of specific facts and ideas and to promote critical thinking and analytical skills. Students who complete all the exercises will have a thorough grasp of the material covered in the text.

Through over twenty years of college teaching, we have worked with a variety of students who have provided insight into this *Study Guide*. Most students enrolled in a Western civilizations course are entering freshmen who need guidance in how to prepare for such a college course. In many instances, classes are so large that instructors cannot give the guidance they would like to provide. Sometimes, students are working and do not have time to meet with instructors. Some students just prefer to work on their own. These are among the factors that have contributed to our preparation of this guide, which we know will be helpful.

Each chapter of the *Study Guide* begins with an overview of the material covered in the chapter followed by an outline. Each chapter contains identification terms, multiple-choice questions, matching items, true/false questions, chronological order exercises, and short-answer and discussion questions. Identification terms allow students to address specific items and examine their significance. In defining identification terms, a student should be able to explain carefully and fully the importance of a person, event, or term. The multiple choice and matching items and true/false questions test students' ability to remember certain facts, events, individuals, trends, and explanations in the text as well as their critical reasoning skills. Chronological order exercises enable students to arrange events often included thematically within the text in correct sequence.

The exercises are designed as building blocks to complement the short-answer and essay questions which show how events, facts, and ideas fit into a proper interpretation of history. Questions break down material into smaller components and reveal how ideas and events are interconnected. They provide an excellent opportunity to analyze information, and students should fully explain answers by giving detailed responses with examples. Short-answer questions are grouped together thematically to provide ideas for longer essays. Some questions specifically address document readings included in the text.

CHAPTER 11

Commerce, Conquest, and Colonization, 1300–1600

The theme in this chapter is how the economic emergence of the western part of Europe occurred. Various parts of the chapter focus on areas that preceded this or were involved in this economic expansion. Mediterranean and Atlantic economies grew and increased as well.

CHAPTER OUTLINE

1. Introduction

2. The Mongols
   a. The rise of the Mongol empire
   b. Europe, the Mongols, and the Far East

3. The rise of the Ottoman Empire
   a. The conquest of Constantinople
   b. War, slavery, and social advancement
   c. Religious conflicts
   d. The Ottomans and Europe

4. Mediterranean colonialism
   a. Silver shortages and the search for African gold
   b. From the Mediterranean to the Atlantic
   c. The technology of ships and navigation
   d. Portugal, Africa, and the sea route to Asia
   e. Artillery and empire
   f. Prince Henry the Navigator
   g. Atlantic colonization and the growth of slavery

5. Europe encounters a New World
   a. The discovery of the New World
   b. The Spanish conquest of America
   c. The profits of empire in the New World

6. Conclusion

IDENTIFY

1. Christopher Columbus
2. Chingiz Khan
3. Timur the Lame
4. Marco Polo
5. Ferdinand Magellan
6. Mehmet II
7. Ottoman slaves
8. conquistadors
9. Bartholomeu Dias
10. Prince Henry the Navigator

MULTIPLE CHOICE

1. With the decline of inner-European expansion, Europe
   a. entered a period in which monarchies concentrated exclusively on domestic issues.
   b. moved east to conquer territories previously ruled by Byzantium.
   c. established sea-based colonies.
   d. embarked on a new period of internal warfare with death rates far worse than the Bubonic Plague.

2. The Mongol ruler who completed the conquest of China was _____.
   a. Chingiz Khan
   b. Qubilai Khan
   c. Timur the Lame
   d. Temujin

3. All of the following are true regarding the Mongols except
   a. they were generally intolerant of other religions.
   b. they brutally killed those who resisted their rule.
   c. they supported trade with European merchants.
   d. they were accomplished cavalrymen.

4. The Ottoman conquest of Constantinople
   a. prevented Europeans from acquiring eastern luxury items.
   b. was the main reason Portugal sought another sea route to Asia.
   c. had a minimal economic effect on western Europe.
   d. both a and b

5. Which of the following is not true regarding slavery in the Ottoman world?
   a. Slaves were predominant in the Ottoman army and administration.
   b. The Ottomans used Christians and Muslims as slaves.
   c. Balkan families provided slave children to pay for an imposed "child tax."
   d. Special schools trained slaves to serve the Ottomans.

6. European colonial and commercial activities in the western Mediterranean and Atlantic world reflected
   a. Europe's increased demand for African gold.
   b. the dominance of the Ottoman Empire in the East.
   c. the conflict between France and Britain over control of the slave trade.
   d. both a and b

7. All of the following technological innovations benefited European sailors in the fifteenth and sixteenth centuries except _____.
   a. quadrants
   b. astrolabes
   c. marine chronometers
   d. compasses

8. All of the following are true about Prince Henry the Navigator except:
   a. stories about his significance to Portuguese exploration appear to be exaggerated.
   b. he was involved in the slave trade.
   c. his main goal was to gain control of the African gold trade.
   d. he made most of his fortune in the spice trade.

9. Native peoples used as workers by the Spanish
   a. turned their Caribbean holdings into productive sugar plantations.
   b. helped them conquer the Aztecs and Inkas.
   c. frequently died of disease and brutal treatment.
   d. all of the above

10. The Spanish conquest of the New World
    a. led directly to a price revolution by accelerating existing inflationary patterns.
    b. required the introduction of slaves to engage in sugar production.
    c. ended the silver shortage in Europe.
    d. all of the above

MATCHING

1. Temujin
2. Marco Polo
3. Mehmet II
4. Battle of Lepanto
5. Canary Islands
6. rutters
7. Prester John
8. Bartholomeu Dias
9. Magellan
10. Pizarro
11. Cortes
12. Potosí

a. conquered the Aztecs
b. conquered the Inkas
c. rounded Africa's southern tip
d. his voyage circumnavigated the globe
e. mythical Christian king in Africa
f. author of *Travels*
g. became Chingiz Khan
h. silver mines in Bolivia
i. Habsburg victory over the Ottomans
j. described coastal landmarks for pilots
k. "jumping off point" for Columbus
l. led the conquest of Constantinople

TRUE/FALSE

1. By the 1520s, Portugal dominated the spice trade.

2. Spain's economic diversity prevented inflation from occurring in the early sixteenth century.

3. Paris was the largest city in Europe by 1600.

4. After conquering Jerusalem and Cairo, Ottoman rulers assumed the title caliph.

5. The Ottomans could count on the support of Orthodox Christians in their wars against the Christian West.

6. The greatest ally of the Ottomans was Persia.

7. The individual most responsible for publicizing awareness of the New World was Queen Isabella.

8. Except in Iberia and Italy, slavery had disappeared from western Europe by the twelfth century.

9. The first Europeans to reach the New World were the Spanish.

10. The Spanish were not initially excited upon learning of the existence of the New World.

PUT THE FOLLOWING ITEMS IN CHRONOLOGICAL ORDER

1. Ottoman ruler assumes title of caliph   _____

2. Battle of Lepanto   _____

3. Qubilai Khan conquers southern China   _____

4. Conquest of Constantinople   _____

5. Magellan's voyage   _____

SHORT ANSWER AND ESSAY QUESTIONS

A. Mongols

1. What impact did the Mongol conquests have on Europe?

2. Trace the expansion of the Mongol empire.

3. Why would *Marco Polo's Description of Java* be of interest to his readers? What do you find of interest in the selection?

B. Ottoman Turks

1. How did the Ottoman Turks benefit from the Mongol expansion?

2. How did the Ottomans increase their power?

3. Explain how the Ottomans differed from their predecessors in Constantinople in their religion and style of government. What did they see as their position in religion and its importance to the state?

4. In the reading *Enslaved Laborers at Potosí*, what was life like for the workers?

5. What factors led to the successful expansion of the Ottoman Empire?

C. Mediterranean colonialism

1. What were the reasons that led to the new Western orientation toward the Atlantic world?

2. Explain how technological changes helped the western Europeans' explorations and colonizations.

3. What were the motives for the voyages of the Portuguese and the Spanish?

4. Explain why the Europeans were so successful in their commercial empires.

5. How were the Portuguese able to control Indian Ocean trade?

D. Europe and the "New World"

1. Examine the impact of the New World silver, both long and short term, on the European economy.

2. How does the selection *Enslaved Native Laborers at Potosí* help you to understand the effect of the silver market on the natives?

3. What other products, besides silver, contributed to the economic relationship between the old and new worlds?

MULTIPLE CHOICE KEY

1. c
2. b
3. a
4. c
5. b
6. a
7. c
8. d
9. c
10. d

MATCHING KEY

1. g
2. f
3. l
4. i
5. k
6. j
7. e
8. c
9. d
10. b
11. a
12. h

TRUE/FALSE KEY

1. T
2. F
3. F
4. T
5. T
6. F
7. F
8. T
9. F
10. T

CHRONOLOGICAL ORDER KEY

3, 4, 5, 1, 2

CHAPTER 12

The Civilization of the Renaissance, c. 1350–1550

This chapter looks at the intellectual and cultural history of the period known as the "Renaissance." The term is used to describe trends in thought, literature, and the arts that emerged between 1350 and 1550.

CHAPTER OUTLINE

1. Introduction

2. The Renaissance and the Middle Ages
   a. Renaissance classicism
   b. Renaissance humanism

3. The Renaissance in Italy
   a. The origins of the Italian Renaissance
   b. The Italian Renaissance: literature and thought
   c. The emergence of textual scholarship
   d. Renaissance Neoplatonism
   e. Machiavelli
   f. The ideal of the courtier

4. The Italian Renaissance: painting, sculpture, and architecture
   a. Renaissance painting in Florence
      i. Leonardo Da Vinci
   b. The Venetian School
   c. Painting in Rome
      i. Raphael
      ii. Michelangelo
   d. Sculpture
      i. Donatello
      ii. Michelangelo
   e. Architecture

5. The waning of the Italian Renaissance

6. The Renaissance in the north
   a. Christian humanism and the northern Renaissance
      i. Desiderius Erasmus
      ii. Sir Thomas More
   b. The decline of Christian humanism
   c. Literature, art, and music, in the northern Renaissance
      i. Painting
      ii. Music

7. Conclusion

IDENTIFY

1. Albrecht Dürer
2. François Rabelais
3. Renaissance humanism
4. Petrarch
5. Leon Battista Alberti
6. Lorenzo Valla
7. *Utopia*
8. Machiavelli
9. Baldassare Castiglione
10. Massacio
11. Leonardo da Vinci
12. Raphael
13. Michelangelo
14. Donatello
15. Desiderius Erasmus

MULTIPLE CHOICE

1. Most scholars today regard the Renaissance as
   a. a time when Europe first became modern and a secular spirit triumphed over medieval Christian culture.
   b. a period that witnessed the rise of new monarchs who no longer felt constrained by medieval notions of rule.
   c. a term best used to describe artistic and literary trends that emerged in Italy between 1350 and 1550 before spreading to northern Europe.
   d. the rebirth of classical Roman society.

2. In comparison with the medieval world,
   a. more literary works from ancient Greece and Rome were available to Renaissance scholars.
   b. Renaissance humanists were less likely to regard ancient texts as confirming basic Christian assumptions.
   c. Renaissance culture was more worldly and secular in spirit.
   d. all of the above

3. Renaissance humanists
   a. promoted the study of logic and metaphysics as a path to understanding God's world.
   b. stressed the study of language, literature, history, and ethics.
   c. generally thought that upper-class women should gain a classical education.
   d. generally sought inward peace through rigid study of Greek in cloister-like communities.

4. The Renaissance began in Italy for all of the following reasons except
   a. the Council of Constance promoted new learning and a greater awareness of the ancient roots of Italian civilization.
   b. Italy enjoyed a significantly urbanized culture.
   c. the Italian upper class was well educated.
   d. Italy's wealth kept scholars from seeking fortunes elsewhere in Europe.

5. Unlike civic humanists, Petrarch's notion of humanism
   a. endorsed a life of government service as the ideal human aspiration.
   b. meant solitary contemplation and withdrawal from worldly affairs.
   c. challenged Italians to unite against foreign invaders.
   d. accepted the basic tenets of scholasticism.

6. In *The Prince*, Machiavelli suggested that a ruler should be judged by
   a. his ability to unite people using Christian principles.
   b. his acceptance of republican ideals and virtues.
   c. the results of his actions.
   d. his commitment to prevailing standards of ethical and moral behavior.

7. All of the following are true of Leonardo da Vinci except
   a. he was a skilled painter, mathematician, inventor, and engineer.
   b. his paintings began the High Renaissance.
   c. he painted the Sistine Chapel.
   d. he sought to accurately imitate nature.

8. Michelangelo is known for all the following except _____.
   a. *The Last Judgement*
   b. *David*
   c. *Descent from the Cross*
   d. *The Virgin of the Rocks*

9. All of the following are reasons for the decline of the Italian Renaissance except
   a. the invasion of Italy by foreign powers.
   b. the Catholic church's attempt to impose doctrinal uniformity.
   c. the decline of Italian wealth.
   d. the exodus of artists and philosophers for Paris.

10. A key distinction between northern Renaissance humanism and Italian Renaissance humanism was that
    a. northern Renaissance humanists placed a greater value on scholasticism.
    b. northern Renaissance humanism reflected a stronger secular orientation.
    c. the writings of Italian Renaissance humanists essentially reflected the views of their patrons.
    d. none of the above

11. Which of the following best describes the humanism of Erasmus?
    a. He intended his writings to promote proper Christian behavior.
    b. His emphasis on Cicero made the Church restrict publication of some of his writings.
    c. He carefully sought to avoid discussion of contemporary Christian practices.
    d. both b and c

12. Thomas More's *Utopia*
    a. examined an ideal Christian community whose laws were based on the Old Testament.
    b. served as an attack on the abuses of his age.
    c. suggested that society's ills could be eliminated if peasants were given private property.
    d. called upon Christians to take up arms against the enemies of the Gospels.

MATCHING

1. Petrarch
2. Alberti
3. Valla
4. Cesare Borgia
5. Castiglione
6. Botticelli
7. Charles V
8. Bruno
9. Dürer
10. Rabelais

a. painted *Birth of Venus*
b. taught how to become a "Renaissance Man"
c. French satirist
d. burned at the stake by the Inquisition
e. endorsed the nuclear family
f. northern Renaissance artist
g. father of Renaissance humanism
h. son of Pope Alexander VI
i. proved that the Donation of Constantine was forged
j. his troops sacked Rome in 1527

TRUE/FALSE

1. It was only during the Renaissance that scholars translated the major works of Virgil into Latin.

2. Italian aristocrats were more urbanized than most of their western European counterparts.

3. Generally, Italian Renaissance scholars were noted for their progressive ideas concerning a woman's status in society.

4. Most of the great painters of the fifteenth century were from Florence.

5. Renaissance architecture disdained medieval architecture and relied exclusively on ancient patterns.

6. Among the reasons for the decline of Christian humanism is the rise of Protestantism.

7. The piano and the harpsichord were developed during the Renaissance.

8. In *Gargantua and Pantagruel*, Rabelais satirized religious practices and superstitions.

9. Machiavelli criticized republican government in his *Discourses on Livy*.

10. Opera was one of the musical innovations developed during the Renaissance.

PUT THE FOLLOWING ITEMS IN CHRONOLOGICAL ORDER

1. Publication of the Index of Forbidden Books _____

2. The sack of Rome by Charles V _____

3. Roman Inquisition established _____

4. Charles VIII's invasion of Italy _____

5. Execution of Sir Thomas More _____

SHORT ANSWER AND ESSAY QUESTIONS

A. Humanism

1. In what new ways did Renaissance writers use classical texts?

2. What is humanism? What was the educational program of the humanists?

3. Using the readings in the text on *The Humanists' Educational Program* find examples of three different traits of humanism. What did each of these writers suggest you should study? Why do you think those subjects were chosen?

4. Why did the Renaissance begin in Italy?

5. What were the characteristics of civic humanism?

6. What does the selection *Some Renaissance Attitudes Toward Women* tell you about the view toward education for women during this period?

7. What are the various views on Machiavelli? Why do you need to consider both Machiavelli's *The Prince* and his *Discourses* to understand him?

B. Italian Renaissance Art

1. What was new about Renaissance art when compared to late medieval art?

2. What are the similarities and differences reflected in the works of artists from different cities? (Make sure you look at the pictures in the textbook and use them as examples when you discuss the artists' works.)

3. Why was Michelangelo regarded as the supreme Renaissance artist?

4. How did Renaissance sculpture differ from medieval sculpture? What similarities do you recognize with the sculpture of the Greeks?

5. Why did the Renaissance decline in Italy around 1550?

C. The Renaissance in the north

1. What was Christian humanism?

2. What are the differences between Christian humanism in the north and the earlier Italian humanism? Use Erasmus' works to illustrate these differences.

3. During the Renaissance what changes took place in the style, theory, and forms of music and its place in society?

D. General questions

1. Consider what made the Renaissance unique.

2. What were the new ways of thinking and approaching intellectual pursuits?

3. How did the northern and Italian Renaissances differ from one another?

MATCHING KEY

1. g
2. e
3. i
4. h
5. b
6. a
7. j
8. d
9. f
10. c

MULTIPLE CHOICE KEY

1. c
2. d
3. b
4. a
5. b
6. c
7. c
8. d
9. d
10. d
11. a
12. b

TRUE/FALSE KEY

1. F
2. T
3. F
4. T
5. F
6. T
7. F
8. T
9. F
10. T

CHRONOLOGICAL ORDER KEY

4, 2, 5, 3, 1

CHAPTER 13 | Reformations of Religion

The focus of this chapter is on the various kinds of religious reformations that occurred during the sixteenth century. These changes in the Christian church were theological but also affected the political states.

CHAPTER OUTLINE

1. Introduction

2. The Lutheran upheaval
   a. Luther's quest for religious certainty
      i. The Reformation begins
      ii. The break with Rome
      iii. The Diet of Worms
      iv. The German princes and the Lutheran reformation

3. The spread of Protestantism
   a. The Reformation in Switzerland
      i. Ulrich Zwingli
      ii. Anabaptism
   b. John Calvin's Reformed theology
      i. Calvinism in Geneva

4. The domestication of the Reformation, 1525–1560
   a. Protestantism and the family
   b. Protestantism and control over marriage

5. The English Reformation
   a. Henry VIII and the break with Rome
   b. Edward VI
   c. Mary Tudor and the restoration of Catholicism
   d. The Elizabethan religious settlement

6. Catholicism transformed
   a. The Catholic Reformation

   b. Saint Ignatius Loyola and the Society of Jesus
   c. Counter-Reformation Christianity

7. Conclusion: The heritage of the Protestant Reformation

IDENTIFY

1. Martin Luther
2. Edward VI
3. Mary Tudor
4. Tetzel
5. Pope Leo X
6. Diet of Worms
7. Elizabeth I
8. Charles V
9. Ulrich Zwingli
10. Anabaptism
11. John Calvin
12. Council of Trent
13. Henry VIII
14. Pope Clement VII
15. Ignatius Loyola

MULTIPLE CHOICE

1. Prior to 1513, young Martin Luther
   a. sought to gain salvation through traditional means.
   b. constantly feared he would never enter heaven.
   c. painstakingly sought ways to undermine traditional Catholic teachings.
   d. both a and b

2. The late Medieval church encouraged the notion that
   a. humans could gain salvation through good works alone.
   b. people could not affect their salvation in any way.
   c. the concept of purgatory was a fiction that needed to be eliminated.
   d. none of the above

3. Luther developed his Ninety-five Theses in response to
   a. the election of Pope Leo X.
   b. the sale of indulgences.
   c. clerical pluralism.
   d. the charge of heresy issued by Leo X.

4. All of the following principles form the basis of Lutheranism except
   a. justification by faith.
   b. the priesthood of all believers.
   c. the primacy of scripture.
   d. that fasting and pilgrimages reflect spiritual perfection.

5. Charles V's holdings included all of the following except _____.
   a. Spain
   b. Naples
   c. Venetia
   d. Austria

6. The Anabaptists left Zwingli's movement over the issue of _____.
   a. the nature of the Eucharist
   b. predestination
   c. infant baptism
   d. all of the above

7. According to John Calvin,
   a. because God has predestined some for salvation, humans can do nothing to alter their fate.
   b. pious behavior may indicate that one has been chosen for salvation.
   c. religious services should be simple and remain free of Catholic symbols and rituals.
   d. all of the above

8. Henry VIII broke with Rome because
   a. of the inspiration he received from Luther's writings.
   b. of the public's response to massive corruption in the monasteries.
   c. his first marriage failed to produce a son.
   d. all of the above

9. After the appointment of Henry VIII as Supreme Head of the Church of England,
   a. Henry organized the church along Lutheran lines.
   b. Archbishop Cranmer immediately adopted Calvinist teachings and simplified church services.
   c. the church essentially remained Catholic in doctrine and practice.
   d. the church declared a pilgrimage to Canterbury a supreme act of piety.

10. Which of the following is correct regarding the Church of England after the death of Henry VIII?
    a. Under Elizabeth the Church of England included both Protestant and Catholic beliefs and practices.
    b. Mary's war with Spain undermined Catholic authority in England.
    c. Edward VI restored Roman authority over the Church of England.
    d. The monasteries were restored despite widespread public outrage.

11. The Council of Trent
    a. refers to the internal Catholic reform movement that altered the Mass.
    b. reaffirmed traditional Catholic doctrines.
    c. accepted Protestant teachings regarding the Eucharist.
    d. is largely regarded as a triumph for the conciliar movement.

12. Saint Ignatius Loyola
    a. created the most militant Catholic organization during the Counter-Reformation.
    b. wrote *The Spiritual Exercises*, a handbook for serving God.
    c. turned the Society of Jesus into a remarkably democratic order.
    d. both a and b

MATCHING

1. Treasury of Merits
2. indulgence
3. Jesuits
4. Tetzel
5. Zwingli
6. Geneva
7. Münster
8. Reformed Church
9. Consistory
10. Ursilines

a. ruled briefly by Anabaptist extremists
b. Calvinist church
c. supervised morality in Geneva
d. storehouse of good deeds
e. forgiveness of penitential obligations
f. sold indulgences for salvation
g. Catholic order for women
h. Society of Jesus
i. organized his religious reforms in Zurich
j. ruled by John Calvin

TRUE/FALSE

1. The suppression of the Peasants' Revolt strengthened the alliance between Lutheranism and the state.

2. Luther disappointed his father by becoming a Dominican friar.

3. At the Diet of Worms, Luther was declared an outlaw although the decree was never enforced.

4. The German nobility regarded Lutheranism as an opportunity to reform the feudal system.

5. Mennonite communities are one of the legacies of Anabaptism.

6. Calvinism was a much more aggressive form of Protestantism than Lutheranism.

7. John Knox "reformed" the church in Scotland.

8. Protestantism differed from Catholicism by approving the sanctity of marital sexuality.

9. The creation of the Index of Forbidden Books reflected the growing intolerance of Protestantism.

10. The Council of Trent eliminated the doctrine of indulgences.

PUT THE FOLLOWING ITEMS IN CHRONOLOGICAL ORDER

1. Opening of the Council of Trent _____

2. Posting of the Ninety-five Theses _____

3. John Calvin gains control of Geneva _____

4. Death of Ulrich Zwingli _____

5. The Diet of Worms _____

SHORT ANSWER AND ESSAY QUESTIONS

A. The importance of Martin Luther

1. What is Luther's view of the "justice of God"? How does this differ from the medieval church's view?

2. How did Luther's view regarding salvation also differ from the medieval church?

3. What were the reasons behind the charges against Luther by Pope Leo X?

4. Explain the three primary theological premises of Luther.

5. What were the reasons for such dissatisfaction with popes, particularly in Germany?

B. Political implications within Germany

1. What problems did Emperor Charles V face in his ability to rule within Germany?

2. How were political rulers able to control or limit religion within their own states?

3. Why did various German princes support Luther's religious practices within their own territories?

C. The spread of Protestantism

1. Why did Switzerland emerge as an important center for sixteenth-century Protestantism?

2. Compare and contrast the theological views of Zwingli and Luther.

3. In his *Institutes of the Christian Religion*, what did Calvin use as the starting point to his theological interpretation?

4. Explain the differences between Luther and Calvin regarding church government.

5. How did the notions of family and marriage change during the Reformation? Why did parents feel they should choose marriage partners for their children?

D. The English Reformation

1. Why did England become a Protestant country?

2. What were Henry VIII's motives for wanting to break his marriage bonds?

3. What problems faced Clement VII in his consideration of Henry VIII's annulment?

4. How did the break between the English church and the church at Rome occur? What were the political components involved in this break?

5. Explain how the theology kept changing in England depending on which of Henry VIII's children was on the throne. What was the final settlement?

F. Catholicism transformed

1. What were the differences between the "Catholic Reformation" and the "Counter-Reformation"?

2. What were the results of the Council of Trent regarding theology or doctrine and the role of both the clergy and the laity? What other changes were a result of decisions made?

3. Examine the growth of the Society of Jesus from its beginning to becoming the "shock troops" of the Counter-Reformation. What were the original goals and the ensuing activities? How do these reflect qualities found in the selection *Obedience as a Jesuit Hallmark*?

MULTIPLE CHOICE KEY

1. d
2. a
3. b
4. d
5. c
6. c
7. d
8. c
9. c
10. a
11. b
12. d

MATCHING KEY

1. d
2. e
3. h
4. f
5. i
6. j
7. a
8. b
9. c
10. g

TRUE/FALSE KEY

1. T
2. F
3. T
4. F
5. T
6. T
7. T
8. T
9. F
10. F

CHRONOLOGICAL ORDER KEY

2, 5, 4, 3, 1

CHAPTER 14 | Religious Wars and State Building, 1540–1660

One theme of this chapter is the connection between religion and political authority. There is also a focus on the reasons that the period between 1540 and 1660 is considered one of the most turbulent in European history. The resulting doubt and uncertainty produced a quest for political understanding and new approaches to literature and art.

CHAPTER OUTLINE

1. Introduction

2. Economic, religious, and political tests
   a. The price revolution
   b. Religious conflicts
   c. Political instability

3. A century of religious wars
   a. The German wars of religion to 1555
   b. The French wars of religion
   c. The revolt of the Netherlands
   d. England and the defeat of the Spanish Armada
   e. The Thirty Years' War

4. Divergent paths: Spain, France, and England, 1600–1660
   a. The decline of Spain
   b. The growing power of France
      i. Cardinal Richelieu
      ii. The Fronde
   c. The English civil war
      i. The origins of the English civil war
      ii. Civil war and Commonwealth
      iii. The restoration of the monarchy

5. The problem of doubt and the quest for certainty
   a. Witchcraft accusations and the power of the state
   b. The search for authority

6. Literature and the arts
   a. Miguel de Cervantes (1547–1616)
   b. Elizabethan and Jacobean drama
   c. Mannerism
   d. Baroque art and architecture
   e. Dutch painting in the "golden age"

7. Conclusion

IDENTIFY

1. Price Revolution
2. Charles V
3. Peace of Augsburg
4. Huguenots
5. Rembrandt van Rijn
6. Henry of Navarre
7. Philip II
8. Spanish Armada
9. Thomas Hobbes
10. Thirty Years' War
11. William Shakespeare
12. Cardinal Richelieu
13. Charles I
14. Oliver Cromwell
15. Gianlorenzo Bernini

MULTIPLE CHOICE

1. All of the following contributed to the Price Revolution except the
   a. increasing demand for food.
   b. influx of bullion from Spanish America.

c. increasing supply of food produced.

d. rising population of Europe.

2. According to the Peace of Augsburg
   a. Charles V reestablished religious unity in the Holy Roman empire.
   b. Charles V divided his holdings among his sons.
   c. within the Holy Roman empire, the ruler of a territory determined the religion of the territory.
   d. Lutheranism was officially recognized as a heresy.

3. The Saint Bartholomew's Day massacre refers to the event after
   a. Catherine de' Medici decided to rule France in her name.
   b. leading Huguenots assembled in Paris for a wedding between Henry of Navarre and Catherine de' Medici's daughter.
   c. King Henry III of France died with no male heirs, thus opening a battle for control of the crown.
   d. Huguenots went on a rampage to start a civil war.

4. The Edict of Nantes
   a. allowed Huguenots to worship freely throughout France.
   b. ended the religious rivalries in France and allowed Henry of Navarre to become king.
   c. limited the rights of Catholics to worship in regions with a Calvinist majority.
   d. granted limited religious freedoms and political rights to French Protestants.

5. Philip II assembled the Spanish Armada
   a. to convince Queen Elizabeth to take his hand in marriage.
   b. because of England's support for the Dutch rebels.
   c. because the Dutch opened the dikes, forcing the Duke of Alva to transport troops by water.
   d. initially to thwart the threat of English pirates to Spanish shipping.

6. France entered the Thirty Years' War
   a. to support the reestablishment of Catholicism throughout the Holy Roman empire.
   b. to test their forces against the mighty Swedish army under Gustavus Adolphus.
   c. to prevent Habsburg forces from winning.
   d. to deal a final death blow to Calvinism in France.

7. The Peace of Westphalia
   a. reflected the growing power of Austrian Habsburgs.
   b. allowed Spain to retake the Netherlands over the protests of France.
   c. turned the Holy Roman empire into a unified military power.
   d. began a period when France emerged as the dominant power on the continent.

8. Cardinal Richelieu's policies served to
   a. strengthen the power of the monarchy.
   b. promote greater religious toleration.
   c. strengthen France economically through overseas conquests.
   d. unite France and Britain against the decaying Spanish empire.

9. English Puritans
   a. resented any attempt to alter the Church of England.
   b. supported efforts to restore some Catholic practices.
   c. wanted Calvinism to triumph in England.
   d. supported the monarchy in the English civil war.

10. Oliver Cromwell's rule in England is best described as _____.
    a. an enlightened republic
    b. a dictatorship
    c. a parliamentary form of government
    d. a religious democracy

11. All of the following are true concerning witchcraft except
    a. accused witches in Protestant countries were almost always treated leniently.
    b. many believed that witches had made a pact with the devil.
    c. authorities employed torture to secure confessions.
    d. witchcraft trials reflected the growing power of the state to protect society.

12. Jean Bodin would have most likely argued that
    a. sovereignty must be vested in an all-powerful monarch.
    b. representative government is essential for protecting citizens' rights.
    c. rulers who became tyrants should be overthrown.
    d. none of the above

MATCHING

1. Huguenots
2. Catherine de' Medici
3. Duke of Alva
4. Gustavus Adolphus
5. Duke of Sully
6. The Fronde
7. Velázquez
8. Protectorate
9. Hobbes
10. Cervantes

a. author of *Leviathan*
b. Baroque master
c. instituted the Council of Blood
d. author of *Don Quixote*
e. French Calvinists
f. began as a revolt against Mazarin's policies
g. the "Lion of the North"
h. Queen mother of France
i. promoted internal improvements in France
j. Cromwell's government

TRUE/FALSE

1. The spread of Calvinism within France benefited from the conversion of several female aristocrats.

2. During the Thirty Years' War, France supported the Catholic forces.

3. The English civil war began after Charles I attempted to have several parliamentary leaders arrested.

4. William Shakespeare was more popular than Christopher Marlowe in Elizabethan England.

5. Michel de Montaigne's *Essays* reflect his skepticism of the benefits of religious toleration.

6. Gianlorenzo Bernini and Peter Brueghel were masters of Mannerism.

7. William of Orange was a diehard Catholic who supported Philip II's attempts to suppress Calvinism in the Netherlands.

8. During the "Protectorate," Cromwell flooded the House of Lords with Puritans.

9. Baroque architecture often was designed to promote Catholic principles.

10. Spain's greatest problems in the seventeenth century were economic.

PUT THE FOLLOWING ITEMS IN CHRONOLOGICAL ORDER

1. Peace of Westphalia _____

2. Saint Bartholomew's Day Massacre _____

3. Spanish Armada _____

4. Beheading of Charles I _____

5. Beginning of Stuart Dynasty _____

SHORT ANSWER AND ESSAY QUESTIONS

A. Economic

1. Explain what brought about soaring prices and the effect of this inflation on society.

2. How did the Price Revolution place new pressures on governments?

B. Religious conflicts

1. What were the basic issues of the German wars of religion that began in 1555? How were these issues resolved?

2. What were the stipulations and guarantees in the Edict of Nantes? How did this change France?

3. Examine Philip II's attitude in relation to the Netherlands.

4. What were the various reasons for the political rebellion in the Netherlands?

5. What were the issues in the Thirty Years' War? Why did it shift from a "religious" civil war to one of international politics?

6. In the selection on *The Destructiveness of the Thirty Years' War,* what were the various kinds of cruelty and destructiveness?

C. Divergent paths: Spain, France, and England, 1600–1660

1. Why was Spain's economy its greatest weakness? What contributed to this economic decline?

2. Explain how the French state was strengthened and centralized by Henry IV and then Richelieu.

3. Compare the reigns of James I and Charles I of England.

4. Compare the views toward the political consequences of the two selections in *Democracy and the English Civil War*. What does each have to say about the role of government?

D. Doubt and certainty

1. Why was there a "desperate search for new foundations upon which to reconstruct some measure of certainty"?

2. Show how witchcraft was linked to both the belief system and the political state. Use the reading *Simplicissimus* to show how it illustrates the acceptance of witchcraft as a reality.

3. Explain the differences between Bodin and Hobbes in their views of government?

4. How did Pascal try to appeal to both intelligence and emotion to convince people of the truth of Christianity?

E. Literature and the arts

1. What are the different facets of human nature represented in the characters in *Don Quixote*?

2. How did Christopher Marlowe and Ben Jonson display human nature?

3. Discuss how Shakespeare's plays illustrate a variety of characteristics of human nature. How did his emphasis change over time?

4. What set El Greco's art apart from that of his contemporaries?

5. What made Dutch painting unique? How could this be seen in its themes? How did this also deal with human nature?

6. Compare and contrast Rubens and Rembrandt in their approach to painting.

MULTIPLE CHOICE KEY

1. c
2. c
3. b
4. d
5. b
6. c
7. d
8. a
9. c
10. b
11. a
12. a

MATCHING KEY

1. e
2. h
3. c
4. g
5. i
6. f
7. b
8. j
9. a
10. d

TRUE/FALSE KEY

1. T
2. F
3. T
4. F
5. F
6. F
7. F
8. F
9. T
10. T

CHRONOLOGICAL ORDER KEY

2, 3, 5, 1, 4

CHAPTER 15 | Absolutism and Empire, 1660–1789

This chapter deals with notions of sovereignty. The dominant kind of sovereignty during this period was absolutism. The chapter explains how it was brought about and how it worked. It explains how the idea of absolutism was linked to empire and the growth of empires. Various other kinds of governments that were alternatives to absolutism are also examined. The chapter also deals with the political theory behind various kinds of government. Finally, the last part of the chapter looks at how government, economics, and colonies were connected in the late seventeenth and early eighteenth centuries.

CHAPTER OUTLINE

1. Introduction

2. The appeal and justification of absolutism

3. Alternatives to absolutism
   a. Limited monarchy: The case of England
      i. The reign of Charles II
      ii. King James II
      iii. The Glorious Revolution
      iv. John Locke and the contract theory of government

4. The absolutism of Louis XIV
   a. Performing royalty at Versailles
   b. Administration and centralization
   c. Louis XIV's religious policies
   d. Colbert and royal finance
   e. The wars of Louis XIV to 1697
   f. The War of the Spanish Succession
   g. The Treaty of Utrecht

5. The remaking of central and eastern Europe
   a. The Habsburg empire
   b. The Rise of Brandenburg-Prussia

6. Autocracy in Russia
   a. The early years of Peter's reign
   b. The transformation of the tsarist state
   c. Peter's foreign policy
   d. Catherine the Great and the partition of Poland

7. Commerce and consumption
   a. Economic growth in the eighteenth century
   b. A world of goods

8. Colonization and trade in the seventeenth century
   a. Spanish colonialism
   b. English colonialism
   c. French colonialism
   d. Dutch colonialism
   e. Contrasting patterns of colonial settlement
   f. Colonial rivalries

9. Colonialism and empire
   a. The "triangular" trade in sugar and spices
   b. The commercial rivalry between Britain and France
   c. War and empire in the eighteenth century world
   d. The American Revolution

10. Conclusion

IDENTIFY

1. Louis XIV
2. Charles II
3. James II

4. The Glorious Revolution
5. John Locke
6. Versailles
7. Jean Baptiste Colbert
8. The Treaty of Utrecht
9. Frederick William, "The Great Elector"
10. Frederick William I
11. Peter I
12. Table of Ranks
13. Catherine the Great
14. triangular trade
15. Treaty of Paris

MULTIPLE CHOICE

1. The theory of absolutism
   a. gave rulers complete sovereignty in matters of law, justice, and taxation.
   b. allowed great, hereditary nobles, working through representative bodies, to limit the authority of kings to tax land.
   c. claimed to be as divinely inspired as a father's absolute authority over his family.
   d. both a and c

2. By 1700, all of the following regions were ruled by absolute monarchs except _____.
   a. Russia
   b. Prussia
   c. England
   d. France

3. One of the ways Louis XIV managed to curtail the power of the nobility was by
   a. exiling his great nobles to French colonies in the Americas.
   b. forcing his great nobles to reside at Versailles for part of the year.
   c. enlisting them as his spies and primary police force.
   d. all of the above

4. The Glorious Revolution had its origins in
   a. a desire by Parliament to restore Catholicism.
   b. an attempt by England's leading barons to subvert Parliament.
   c. the fear that a Catholic dynasty would eliminate Protestantism.
   d. both b and c

5. According to John Locke
   a. absolutism was the best guide to restore order and create prosperity.
   b. government was designed to protect life, liberty, and property.
   c. government should redistribute property to the landless to avoid social revolution.
   d. citizens had no right to overthrow absolute monarchs.

6. The League of Augsburg
   a. sought to preserve a balance of power in Europe.
   b. was an attempt to crush the spread of Catholicism in England.
   c. settled the issue regarding a Spanish successor to Charles II through wise diplomacy.
   d. allowed the Habsburgs to extend their authority over the United Provinces.

7. The Treaty of Utrecht allowed for all of the following except
   a. Austrian control of part of northern Italy.
   b. Spanish control over the slave trade.
   c. British control over Gibraltar and several former French colonies in the New World.
   d. Louis XIV's grandson to be king of Spain.

8. The nobility under Frederick the Great Elector
   a. was allowed to enserf peasants.
   b. served as the officer corps of his army.
   c. saw their taxes increase dramatically.
   d. both a and b

9. Peter the Great's policies of "westernization" were essentially aimed at
   a. increasing agricultural productivity through enserfment of the peasants.
   b. enhancing the prestige of the Russian orthodox church by introducing new bishoprics.
   c. increasing Russian military power.
   d. turning Russia into the most elegant and culturally refined great power in Europe.

10. Significant economic developments in the eighteenth century included
    a. the growth of urban manufacturing.
    b. the introduction of new crops and methods of farming.
    c. the increasing use of rural labor in textile production.
    d. all of the above

11. The most profitable commodity (commodities) imported into England from its colonies in the New World and Asia was/were _____.
    a. tobacco
    b. slaves
    c. potatoes
    d. sugar

12. The triangular trade primarily involved the trans-Atlantic shipping and sale of _____.
    a. fish and furs
    b. sugar and slaves
    c. cotton, sugar, and tobacco
    d. both a and b

MATCHING

1. William of Orange
2. Tories
3. John Locke
4. Coercive Acts
5. Quietists
6. Jansenists
7. Jean Baptiste Colbert
8. Habsburgs
9. Frederick William I
10. Duma

a. practiced personal mysticism
b. wrote *Two Treatises of Government*
c. Russian national assembly
d. Dutch ruler
e. punished Massachusetts
f. supported Charles II
g. transformed Prussia
h. Louis XIV's finance minister
i. strictly adhered to the doctrine of predestination
j. rulers of Austria and Hungary

TRUE/FALSE

1. One of the appeals of absolutism was its promise to restore order and stability after years of turmoil.

2. In Protestant countries, Protestant churches maintained a considerable degree of independence under absolute monarchs.

3. By the 1670s, Charles II patterned his reign after the absolutism of Louis XIV.

4. The Glorious Revolution formally united England and Scotland.

5. Unlike other absolute monarchs, Louis XIV promoted religious toleration to strengthen his hold on France.

6. With the weakening of Ottoman power, Brandenburg-Prussia became Austria's main rival in central Europe.

7. The goal of Peter the Great's foreign policy was to gain warm water ports for his navy.

8. Catherine the Great is regarded as an enlightened monarch because of the extensive social reforms she enacted during her reign.

9. By the beginning of the nineteenth century, Poland had disappeared from the map of Europe.

10. Early English North American colonists made significant strides in converting American Indians to Protestantism.

PUT THE FOLLOWING ITEMS IN CHRONOLOGICAL ORDER

1. Peace of Nystad   _____

2. Treaty of Utrecht   _____

3. Glorious Revolution   _____

4. Founding of Jamestown   _____

5. Treaty of Paris   _____

SHORT ANSWER AND ESSAY QUESTIONS

A. The appeal and justification of absolutism

1. What were the aims of absolutist rulers?

2. What problems did rulers encounter in becoming absolute? In what ways did they overcome these?

3. In *Absolutism and Patriarchy,* how does Bossuet support absolutism?

B. Alternatives to absolutism

1. What made the English style of government unique? How did this come about?

2. Compare the reigns of Charles II and James II in England.

3. Describe the events of the Glorious Revolution. What changes occurred in the English government as a result?

4. Discuss John Locke's theory of government. Explain his concept of how government originated and developed and its resulting form. How does Locke's theory differ from absolutism?

C. Absolutism and Louis XIV

1. How did Louis XIV strengthen his control over France?

2. How did Louis XIV bring the nobles under control and reduce their power?

3. Why did Louis XIV think it was necessary to control religion? Explain how he accomplished this goal.

4. Explain how Jean Baptiste Colbert's economic policy strengthened Louis XIV's absolutism. Why are these policies a good example of mercantilism?

5. In the selection *Mercantilism and War,* how does Colbert illustrate how mercantilism supports Louis XIV's policies of war?

6. Compare and contrast the wars of Louis XIV in terms of their objectives, opponents, and outcomes. Did the wars' long-term results accomplish Louis's goals?

7. What were the stipulations of the Treaty of Utrecht? What was its impact on the balance of power between and among European states?

D. Remaking of central and eastern Europe

1. What changes were behind the growing power of Prussia?

2. What were the problems and limitations the Habsburg emperors had in trying to centralize their power?

3. What were the contributions of each of the Prussian rulers (Frederick William, Frederick I, and Frederick William I) in building an absolutist state?

4. How did Peter the Great make Russia into a great European power?

5. How did Peter the Great bring the nobility under his control? How did he try to "westernize" the nobility?

6. What were Peter the Great's successes in foreign policy? How did Catherine add to the territories of Russia? In what directions did this expansion occur?

7. What were the reasons behind the partition of Poland?

E. Economic

1. What contributed to population growth in the countryside and cities?

2. How did developments in trade and manufacturing contribute to the rising prosperity of northwest Europe?

3. Describe the emerging consumer goods market.

F. Colonization and trade

1. How did English colonists try to gain profits? How did this differ from the efforts of the French and Spanish?

2. What new products came from the various colonies that belonged to the European powers?

3. How were joint-stock companies organized? What was innovative about these organizations?

4. What was the model of colonization of the French and Spanish? How did the English model differ? What were the reasons for these differences?

G. Colonialism and empire

1. What was "triangular" trade? What did traders at each of the three points gain? Give an example of how it worked using two colonial powers.

2. How valuable was colonial commerce to the European states?

3. In colonial trade, what was the link between the European governments and the merchants? How did this lead to advantages for the British over the French?

4. Explain how the British and French competition in colonial efforts involved various conflicts of war.

H. The American Revolution

1. How did the British government treat complaints of their colonists in North America?

MULTIPLE CHOICE KEY

1. d
2. c
3. b
4. c
5. b
6. a
7. b
8. d
9. c
10. d
11. d
12. b

MATCHING KEY

1. d
2. f
3. b
4. e
5. a
6. i
7. h
8. j
9. g
10. c

TRUE/FALSE KEY

1. T
2. F
3. T
4. F
5. F
6. T
7. T
8. F
9. T
10. F

CHRONOLOGICAL ORDER KEY

4, 3, 2, 1, 5

CHAPTER 16 | The Scientific Revolution

The theme of this chapter is the scientific revolution. This chapter defines what it was and explains the intellectual environment that produced it, then focuses on the intellectual changes that it produced. These changes provided a new approach to understanding the natural world.

CHAPTER OUTLINE

1. Introduction

2. The intellectual roots of the scientific revolution

3. A revolution in astronomy
   a. The Copernican revolution
   b. Tycho's System and Kepler's Laws
   c. New heavens, new earth, and worldly politics: Galileo Galilei (1564–1642)

4. Methods for a new philosophy: Bacon and Descartes
   a. Bacon and Descartes

5. The power of method and the force of curiosity: Seventeenth-century experimenters
   a. Science societies and the State
   b. "And all was Light": Isaac Newton

6. Conclusion

IDENTIFY

1. Christian nominalism
2. Aristotle
3. Copernicus
4. Tycho Brahe
5. Johannes Kepler
6. Galileo
7. Cardinal Bellarmine
8. Francis Bacon
9. Rene Descartes
10. Mechanists
11. Royal Society of England
12. Isaac Newton

MULTIPLE CHOICE

1. According to the text, the scientific revolution involved three changes. Which of the following is not one of them?
   a. the confirmation of the sun-centered universe
   b. the creation of a new physics
   c. the rejection of religion by the scientific community
   d. the development of a new method of investigation

2. Roots of the scientific revolution could be found in all of the following except
   a. the commitment to naturalism displayed by medieval artists and sculptors.
   b. the increased interest in the nature of light.
   c. an increasing openness in religion brought about by the Protestant Reformation.
   d. the work of the nominalists, which allowed for discussions of the natural world without referencing theology.

3. Renaissance humanists influenced the rise of modern science
   a. through Neoplatonism, which prompted them to seek ideal forms and structures.
   b. by emphasizing the importance of physics and mathematics.
   c. through their extensive observations of planetary motion.
   d. none of the above

4. The two most important ancient sources for medieval astronomers were _____.
   a. Copernicus and Ptolemy
   b. Aristotle and Plato
   c. Aristotle and Ptolemy
   d. Plato and Ptolemy

5. Copernicus believed
   a. that God could not have created a universe as cluttered and confusing as Ptolemy's calculations suggested.
   b. that he produced a better understanding of God's handiwork.
   c. that the earth moved around the sun in an elliptical fashion.
   d. both a and b

6. Johannes Kepler
   a. believed that everything created by God was based on mathematical laws.
   b. developed laws of planetary motion.
   c. disputed a couple of Copernicus's findings regarding planetary motion.
   d. all of the above

7. Galileo wrote all of the following except _____.
   a. *The New Instrument of Heliocentrism*
   b. *A Dialogue Between the Two Great World Systems*
   c. *Letter to the Grand Duchess Christina di Medici*
   d. *The Starry Messenger*

8. The Inquisition dealt with Galileo by
   a. trying him for heresy and burning him at the stake.
   b. ignoring him and burning his writings.
   c. forcing him to recant his beliefs and placing him under house arrest.
   d. challenging him to debate the leading Catholic astronomers.

9. Both Bacon and Descartes
   a. agreed on the necessity of questioning past knowledge.
   b. argued that cooperation between researchers is of limited validity.
   c. believed that truth is best gained by reasoning out from a set of principles.
   d. none of the above

10. Newton explained motion throughout the universe through his law of _____.
    a. inertia
    b. universal gravitation
    c. planetary motion
    d. particle acceleration

MATCHING

1. Archimedes
2. Ptolemy
3. Copernicus
4. Brahe
5. Bellarmine
6. Bacon
7. Descartes
8. Harvey
9. Hooke
10. Newton

a. practitioner of the inductive method
b. Dane who collected extensive astronomical data
c. microscope pioneer
d. described the circulation of the blood
e. ancient Greek authority on planetary motion
f. wrote *Principia Mathematica*
g. critic of the Copernican theory
h. wrote *On the Revolution of Heavenly Spheres*
i. "I think, therefore I am"
j. influenced Renaissance mechanists

TRUE/FALSE

1. The scientific revolution benefited from the emphasis on science education stressed by Renaissance humanists.

2. One of the reasons church officials denied the notion of a sun-centered universe was because it appeared to contradict certain passages in the Bible.

3. The scientific revolution profited from increased collaboration between Renaissance artisans and intellectuals.

4. Problems with the European calendar spurred Copernicus's astronomical observations.

5. Tycho Brahe's calculations proved Copernicus's notion of a sun-centered universe.

6. Bacon and Descartes used the same methods to gain knowledge of the world.

7. Descartes' philosophical speculations encouraged researchers to rely less on mathematics and more on intuition.

8. Newton's discoveries proved that the earth was a perfect circle.

9. Because of their findings, most of the natural philosophers and mechanists ultimately abandoned religion.

10. The Royal Society was created and funded by French monarchs to promote awareness of the new astronomy.

PUT THE FOLLOWING ITEMS IN CHRONOLOGICAL ORDER

1. Creation of the Royal Society   _____

2. Publication of *Discourse on Method*   _____

3. Publication of *On the Revolution of Heavenly Spheres*   _____

4. Publication of *Principia Mathematica* _____

5. Publication of *The Starry Messenger* _____

SHORT ANSWER AND ESSAY QUESTIONS

A. Intellectual roots

1. What were the intellectual roots of the scientific revolution?
2. Explain the differences between Ptolemy's view of the universe and Copernicus' view of the universe.
3. How did Tycho and Kepler build on Copernicus' theory?

B. Galileo

1. Discuss the contributions of Galileo to the scientific revolution both in theoretical and in practical terms.
2. How did Galileo perceive of the relationship between science and religion? Use the selection on "Galileo on Nature, Scripture, and Truth" to help explain this relationship.
3. How did Galileo bring himself into conflict with powerful opponents?
4. Why was the Roman church so concerned with Galileo's work? Look again at "Galileo on Nature, Scripture, and Truth" and assess if you think this was a valid defense.
5. What were Galileo's two great legacies?

C. Natural philosophy

1. How were Bacon and Descartes alike in their intellectual views?
2. What were the philosophical differences between Bacon and Descartes?

D. Science

1. What were the contributions of the Cartesians' use of deductive reasoning?
2. What were the contributions of William Harvey, Robert Boyle, and Robert Hooke?
3. Discuss the career of Isaac Newton. In the essay explain what he contributed to and how he transformed the discipline of science.

4. What were the practical consequences of Newton's intellectual synthesis?
5. Why was Newton's explanation of motion so important?
6. How did natural philosophers' views of the search for answers about the physical world change?
7. How did this new way of thinking bring new beliefs?

MULTIPLE CHOICE KEY

1. c
2. c
3. a
4. c
5. d
6. d
7. a
8. c
9. a
10. b

MATCHING KEY

1. j
2. e
3. h
4. b
5. g
6. a
7. i
8. d
9. c
10. f

TRUE/FALSE KEY

1. F
2. T
3. T
4. T
5. F
6. F
7. F
8. F
9. F
10. F

CHRONOLOGICAL ORDER KEY

3, 5, 2, 1, 4

CHAPTER 17 | The Enlightenment

This chapter focuses on the intellectual movement known as the Enlightenment. Once it has examined the movement, it will show how this led to a reinterpretation of a view of empire. The chapter will also show the Enlightenment's influence on various aspects of society and culture. When you are answering the short answer and essay questions, make sure, when appropriate, to use writers and their works as examples.

CHAPTER OUTLINE

1. Introduction

2. The foundations of the Enlightenment

3. The world of the *philosophes*
   a. Voltaire
   b. Montesquieu
   c. Diderot and the *Encyclopedia*

4. Internationalization of Enlightenment themes
   a. Enlightenment themes: humanitarianism and toleration
   b. Economics, government, and administration

5. Empire and Enlightenment
   a. Slavery and the Atlantic world
   b. Exploration and the Pacific world
   c. The impact of scientific missions

6. Nature, gender, and Enlightenment radicalism: Rousseau and Wollstonecraft
   a. The world of Rousseau
   b. The world of Wollstonecraft

7. The Enlightenment and eighteenth-century culture
   a. The book trade
   b. High culture, new elites, and the "Public Sphere"
      i. Salons
   c. Middle-class culture and reading

d. Popular culture: urban and rural
e. Eighteenth-century music
   i. Bach and Handel
   ii. Hayden and Mozart
   iii. Opera

8. Conclusion

IDENTIFY

1. philosophes
2. John Locke
3. Voltaire
4. Baron de Montesquieu
5. Denis Diderot
6. Cesare Beccaria
7. Moses Mendelssohn
8. Adam Smith
9. Jean-Jacques Rousseau
10. Mary Wollstonecraft
11. the book trade
12. salons
13. Johann Sebastian Bach
14. George Frideric Handel
15. Wolfgang Amadeus Mozart

MULTIPLE CHOICE

1. In his *Essay Concerning Human Understanding*, John Locke argued that
   a. all knowledge is implanted in humans by God.
   b. all knowledge comes from sense experience.
   c. one's environment helps shape one's character.
   d. both b and c

2. Historians have called the Enlightenment a "cultural project" because
   a. the philosophes were the first philosophers to base their findings on reason.
   b. of the philosophes' determination to spread knowledge and promote open, public debate.
   c. of the philosophes' acceptance of democracy as the ideal form of government.
   d. all of the above

3. Voltaire
   a. admired British culture and political institutions.
   b. wanted to eliminate all forms of repression, fanaticism, and bigotry.
   c. particularly despised religious intolerance.
   d. all of the above

4. In the *Spirit of Laws*, Montesquieu
   a. described the observations of two Turkish travelers to France.
   b. described different forms of government along with their virtues and shortcomings.
   c. explained his impression of the enlightened nature of the French monarchy.
   d. called the ideal form of government a democratic republic.

5. Eighteenth-century Europeans who wished to discover the latest scientific and philosophical developments would be advised to consult
   a. Voltaire's *Candide*.
   b. Diderot's *Encyclopedia*.
   c. Rousseau's *Social Contract*.
   d. Rousseau's *Émile*.

6. Cesare Beccaria
   a. thought punishment should be administered only to maintain social order and prevent crime.
   b. supported the death penalty and torture in capital cases.
   c. regarded public executions as valid efforts to deter crime.
   d. all of the above

7. Adam Smith's economic ideas
   a. supported governmental involvement in the economy.
   b. regarded monopolies as preferable to economic competition.
   c. suggested individuals should pursue their own economic interests.
   d. implied that government should assist the poor by redistributing land.

8. Rousseau was regarded as a particularly radical thinker because he
   a. championed the superiority of enlightened monarchy.
   b. was among the first to discuss popular sovereignty and democracy.
   c. thought that children should be given a classical education that emphasized religious morality.
   d. bolstered the relationship between private property and hereditary monarchy.

9. According to Rousseau, the aim of education should be to
   a. make men morally autonomous and good citizens.
   b. encourage rational thought in children at an early age.
   c. teach women to become much more than just wives and mothers.
   d. encourage children to read the great works of Western literature.

10. One of the distinguishing features of the salon was
    a. the presence of members of the lower classes in attendance.
    b. the elaborate, secret rituals that surrounded their gatherings.
    c. their ability to influence monarchs to adopt enlightened agendas.
    d. the prominent role of the women who organized them.

11. The most popular new literary form in the eighteenth century was the _____.
    a. short story
    b. epic poem
    c. novel
    d. tragedy

12. Johann Sebastian Bach
    a. popularized the musical form later known as the symphony.
    b. regarded his compositions as religious expressions of his devout Catholicism.
    c. is best remembered for his operatic compositions.
    d. wrote music for Sunday and holiday church services.

MATCHING

1. philosophe
2. Wollstonecraft
3. Lessing
4. Mendelssohn
5. physiocrats
6. Cook
7. Mozart
8. Haydn
9. Austen
10. Handel

a. promoted Enlightenment ideas among Jews
b. father of the symphony
c. explored the South Pacific
d. composed his first symphony at age nine
e. author of *Pride and Prejudice*
f. master of the Oratorio
g. free thinker
h. supported women's rights
i. supported *laissez-faire* policies
j. author of *Nathan the Wise*

TRUE/FALSE

1. Almost all Enlightenment intellectuals optimistically believed in human progress through education.

2. One of Voltaire's greatest accomplishments was to endorse empiricism and the scientific method.

3. Rousseau's support of "checks and balances" as outlined in the *Social Contract* influenced the formation of the early government of the United States.

4. In order to avoid controversy, Diderot refused to include articles critical of religious practices in his *Encyclopedia*.

5. Philosophes universally condemned slavery in the Americas because it was based on racial supremacy.

6. Rousseau's concept of the general will referred to the common interests shared by a community.

7. Mary Wollstonecraft believed that European civilization and culture prepared women to be dependent on men.

8. Very little literature was written to appeal to middle-class women.

9. The major musical form to originate during the Enlightenment was the opera.

10. The world's first daily newspapers were printed in Moscow.

PUT THE FOLLOWING ITEMS IN CHRONOLOGICAL ORDER

1. Publication of *The Wealth of Nations* _____

2. Publication of *Essay Concerning Human Understanding* _____

3. Publication of *Émile* _____

4. Publication of *Spirit of Laws* _____

5. Publication of *On Crimes and Punishments* _____

SHORT ANSWER AND ESSAY QUESTIONS

A. Foundations of the Enlightenment

1. What were the basic characteristics of Enlightenment writings?
2. Which of Locke's views provided a foundation for many of the Enlightenment thinkers?
3. What was the goal of Enlightenment writers? How did they expect this would be accomplished?

B. The World of the philosophes

1. What themes did Voltaire discuss in his writings?
2. What was Voltaire's view regarding religion?
3. Explain the views of three of the Enlightenment writers concerning politics.
4. What topics were of interest to the Enlightenment writers? Give examples from various works.

C. Internationalization of Enlightenment themes

1. What were the international themes of the Enlightenment thinkers? Give examples of each of these themes by at least one writer.
2. What were the views of the Enlightenment writers regarding religion and religious toleration? Use specific examples to support your statement.
3. What were the economic views of the Enlightenment writers, especially Adam Smith?
4. Compare the economic ideas of Adam Smith concerning the effects of discovering the Americas with Raynal's view as found in the selection "The Impact of the New World on Enlightenment Thinkers."
5. What does the selection "Slavery and the Enlightenment" tell you about the philosophes' view of slavery?
6. How did the Enlightenment writers' views of the Pacific cultures fall into an inquiry about "civilization" and "human nature"?

D. Rousseau

1. What views did Rousseau share with other Enlightenment writers? How did he differ in his beliefs?
2. Explain Rousseau's core ideas of "natural law," "sovereign" society, and "general will" found in his *Social Contract*. How are these illustrated in the excerpt in the textbook?
3. Compare the ideas on education in Rousseau's *Émile* to Locke's *Essay on Human Understanding*.
4. Compare and consider the period's views on women's education by examining the selections from Rousseau's *Émile* to the selections from Madame de Stael and Mary Wollstonecraft. [Reading: *Rousseau and his Readers*.] What does this tell you about the usual position of women in eighteenth-century society?

E. Culture

1. Why did the expansion of the book trade and "print culture" have such a connection to Enlightenment ideas?
2. Explain how ideas circulated in both public and private spheres.
3. What were the reading materials and interests of the middle class?
4. Within various levels of society, what were the means used for an exchange of ideas?

5. Examine the differences between various levels of society at the beginning of the eighteenth century.

F. Eighteenth-century music

1. What were the principles behind compositions written in the "Classical style"?
2. What were the various styles of music during the eighteenth century? What composers are associated with each style?
3. What were the various ways composers financed themselves?

MATCHING KEY

1. g
2. h
3. j
4. a
5. i
6. c
7. d
8. b
9. e
10. f

MULTIPLE CHOICE KEY

1. d
2. b
3. d
4. b
5. b
6. a
7. c
8. b
9. a
10. d
11. c
12. d

TRUE/FALSE KEY

1. T
2. T
3. F
4. F
5. F
6. T
7. T
8. F
9. F
10. F

CHRONOLOGICAL ORDER KEY

2, 4, 3, 5, 1

CHAPTER 18 | The French Revolution

This chapter is about the French Revolution of 1789 and its aftermath. After 1789 the revolutionary period went through several different forms of government, ending in Napoleon Bonaparte's dictatorship and empire. You will need to keep in mind the various changes in government and what each represented. You should also pay attention to the international aspects of this revolutionary period.

CHAPTER OUTLINE

1. Introduction

2. The French Revolution: An overview

3. The coming of the revolution

4. The destruction of the Old Regime
   a. First stages of the French Revolution
      i. Popular revolts
   b. The National Assembly and the liberal revolution

5. A new stage: popular revolution
   a. War
   b. The Jacobins
   c. The Reign of Terror

6. From the terror to Bonaparte: The Directory
   a. Why did the Directory fail?
   b. The Haitian Revolution

7. Napoleon and imperial France
   a. Consolidating authority: 1799–1804
   b. Law, education, and a new elite
   c. In Europe as in France: Napoleon's wars of expansion

8. The return to war and Napoleon's defeat: 1806–1815

9. Conclusion

IDENTIFY

1. Louis XVI
2. Estates-General
3. The National Assembly
4. The Bastille
5. The Great Fear
6. The Civil Constitution of the Clergy
7. The Declaration of the Rights of Man
8. Edmund Burke
9. Jacobins
10. The Reign of Terror
11. Maximilian Robespierre
12. Napoleon Bonaparte
13. The Haitian Revolution
14. The Napoleonic Code
15. The *Grande Armée*

MULTIPLE CHOICE

1. The French Revolution was preceded by all of the following except
   a. Louis XVI's decision to turn France into a constitutional monarchy.
   b. a general rise in prices.
   c. a series of poor harvests and a rise in unemployment.
   d. an increase in the national debt.

2. The most important reason for the outbreak of the French Revolution was
   a. a diplomatic crisis following the end of the American Revolution.
   b. an economic crisis.
   c. peasant revolts inspired by the writings of Rousseau.
   d. the threat of foreign invasion.

3. The main reason for the formation of the National Assembly was
   a. a disagreement between the First and Second Estates over the role of the church.
   b. a disagreement over voting.
   c. an alliance between the Second and the Third Estates over tax reform.
   d. the personal intervention of Louis XVI, who demanded the abolition of feudal privileges.

4. The Declaration of the Rights of Man
   a. became the preamble to France's constitution in 1791.
   b. championed freedom of speech and equality before the law.
   c. turned the clergy into a state-owned institution.
   d. both a and b

5. The Civil Constitution of the Clergy
   a. required church officials to swear allegiance to France.
   b. was greeted by the pope as a progressive initiative.
   c. was supported without reservations throughout rural France.
   d. both a and c

6. Delegates in the National Convention of 1792
   a. declared France a Republic.
   b. were more radical than previous members of the Assembly.
   c. included a majority of aristocrats and monarchists.
   d. both a and b

7. All of the following were accomplished by the National Convention except the
   a. abolition of slavery in French colonies.
   b. abolition of primogeniture.
   c. restoration of papal control over the church.
   d. confiscation of property for redistribution to the lower classes.

8. The individual most responsible for expanding the Reign of Terror was _____.
   a. Danton
   b. Marat
   c. Robespierre
   d. Corday

9. Most individuals killed during the Reign of Terror were _____.
   a. nobles
   b. commoners
   c. clergy
   d. none of the above

10. All of the following are true regarding Napoleon except
    a. he was born in Sicily.
    b. he overthrew the government in 1799.
    c. his government improved tax collection.
    d. he established a system of high schools to train civil servants.

11. According to the Napoleonic Code,
    a. all feudal privileges were abolished.
    b. husbands held considerable authority over their wives.
    c. craft guilds gained additional rights.
    d. both a and b

12. Napoleon's *Grande Armée*
    a. encountered stiff resistance in Spain from guerilla fighters.
    b. was composed mostly of non-French troops.
    c. was devastated by the Russian campaign.
    d. both b and c

MATCHING

1. First Estate
2. Second Estate
3. Third Estate
4. physiocrats
5. Great Fear
6. Olympe de Gouges
7. Jacobins
8. Directory
9. Committee of Public Safety
10. L'Ouverture
11. *lycées*
12. Waterloo

a. promoted equal rights for women
b. Napoleon's final defeat
c. high schools
d. overthrown by Napoleon
e. uprisings in the countryside
f. leader of the Haitian Revolution
g. all those not in the First and Second Estates
h. the nobility
i. radical revolutionaries
j. urged tax reform
k. implemented the Reign of Terror
l. the clergy

TRUE/FALSE

1. The first stage of the French Revolution turned France into a constitutional monarchy.

2. With the Tennis Court Oath, the Third Estate abolished the monarchy.

3. One route to joining the Second Estate was to purchase a title of nobility.

4. Prior to the gathering of the Estates-General, Louis XVI had already intended to reform the tax system.

5. The French Revolution gave civil rights to both Protestants and Jews.

6. The first stage of the French Revolution went largely unnoticed outside of France.

7. Edmund Burke was one of the staunchest supporters of the revolution in France.

8. During the October Days, women of Paris marched to Versailles to seize the Bastille.

9. Throughout his conquered territories, Napoleon attempted to institute revolutionary ideas such as the abolition of privileges.

10. Britain's control of the seas plagued Napoleon's Continental System.

PUT THE FOLLOWING ITEMS IN CHRONOLOGICAL ORDER

1. Fall of the Bastille   _____

2. Execution of Robespierre   _____

3. Battle of Waterloo   _____

4. Execution of Louis XVI   _____

5. Napoleon becomes emperor   _____

6. Formation of the National Assembly   _____

7. Convening of the Estates-General   _____

8. Napoleon invades Russia   _____

SHORT ANSWER AND ESSAY QUESTIONS

A. Background for the French Revolution

1. How was society divided before the revolution?
2. What were the causes of the French Revolution?
3. What were the grievances of the peasants before the outbreak of the French Revolution?

B. The destruction of the Old Regime

1. Once the Estates-General was called, what were the various issues in the government and in the country, both urban and rural, that it had to address?
2. What brought about the three popular uprisings of 1789? How were they alike and in what ways did they differ?
3. What were the goals of the revolution as set forth in the *Declaration of the Rights of Man and Citizen*?
4. Consider the following in the selection from the *Declaration of the Rights of Man*:
   a. What ideals of the Enlightenment are found in this document?
   b. What ideas are similar to the American Declaration of Independence?
5. How does Olympe de Gouges make her case in the selection from *Declaration of the Rights of Women*?
6. Why did the National Assembly's attempt to reform the church encounter difficulty?

C. Radical stage

1. What were the drastic changes between the first and second stages of the French Revolution? Why did these occur?
2. What were the reasons various groups opposed the revolution at this stage?
3. How did the Jacobins gain and maintain their control of the government? Why do you think they were able to do so?
4. What were the challenges to the Committee of Public Safety?

D. Napoleon

1. What was the form of government of the Directory? What were the problems this government faced? Why did the Directory fail?
2. How did Haiti gain its independence? Who were the leaders in this movement and what was the role of each?
3. How did Napoleon become so powerful? Examine both his military and his political successes.
4. Consider the attitude toward women solidified in the Napoleonic Code in conjunction with the earlier selection by Mary Wollstonecraft. What do these tell you about attitudes toward women?
5. What were the effects of Napoleon on the various states he had under his control? How is this illustrated in his *Two Letters from Napoleon*?
6. What were the ramifications of the Continental System that led to Napoleon's downfall?
7. What were Napoleon's reasons for invading Russia? How did this contribute to his downfall?

E. Overall

1. What were the long-term results and legacies of the French Revolution?
2. Trace the various changes in forms of government from the *Ancien Régime* to the fall of Napoleon.

MULTIPLE CHOICE KEY

1. a
2. b
3. b
4. d
5. a
6. d
7. c
8. c
9. b

10. a
11. d
12. d

MATCHING KEY

1. l
2. h
3. g
4. j
5. e
6. a
7. i
8. d
9. k
10. f
11. c
12. b

TRUE/FALSE KEY

1. T
2. F
3. T
4. T
5. T
6. F
7. F
8. F
9. T
10. T

CHRONOLOGICAL ORDER KEY

7, 6, 1, 4, 2, 5, 8, 3

CHAPTER 19 | The Industrial Revolution and Nineteenth-Century Society

This chapter deals with the Industrial Revolution and its economic and social consequences. The chapter begins by tracing the events of the Industrial Revolution and the reasons why it was so revolutionary. It shows how the new economic system produced a cultural shift. The focus on the social history of various classes shows how these groups developed and changed as a result of the Industrial Revolution.

CHAPTER OUTLINE

1. Introduction

2. The Industrial Revolution in Britain, 1760–1850
   a. Innovation in textile industries
   b. Coal and iron
   c. The coming of railways

3. The Industrial Revolution on the Continent
   a. Population
   b. Industrialization after 1850
   c. Industry and empire

4. The social consequences of industrialization
   a. Life on the land: the peasantry
   b. The urban landscape
      i. Industry and environment in the nineteenth century

5. Social Change: the middle classes
   a. Private life and middle-class identity
   b. Gender and the cult of domesticity
   c. "Passionless": gender and sexuality
   d. Middle-class life in public
   e. Working-class life
      i. Working women in the industrial landscape
   f. A life apart: "class" consciousness

6. Conclusion

IDENTIFY

1. causes
2. Great Famine
3. flying shuttle
4. spinning jenny
5. water frame
6. mule
7. cotton gin
8. Factory Acts
9. Thomas Newcomen
10. James Watt
11. navvies
12. Cult of Domesticity

MULTIPLE CHOICE

1. The industrialization of Britain occurred because
   a. it had ample supplies of coal.
   b. it had a developed canal system.
   c. it had an efficient and productive commercialized agricultural system.
   d. all of the above

2. Samuel Compton's mule
   a. was the first locomotive.
   b. combined features of both the water frame and spinning jenny.
   c. pumped water out of coal mines.
   d. none of the above

3. The invention that dramatically increased the production of cotton was the _____.
   a. flying shuttle
   b. water frame
   c. cotton gin
   d. none of the above

4. James Watt is credited with
   a. developing the punch time cards for workers in factories.
   b. improving iron production in northern England.
   c. developing a more efficient steam engine.
   d. successfully petitioning the House of Commons to fund canal construction.

5. All of the following are correct except
   a. railway construction fueled a demand for iron production.
   b. railway construction frequently involved both public and private financing.
   c. railway construction required only a small number of workers because of increased mechanization.
   d. railway construction increased the need for engineering expertise.

6. All of the following delayed the industrialization of continental Europe except _____.
   a. internal tolls and tariffs in much of central Europe
   b. the wars of the French Revolution and Napoleon
   c. underdeveloped transportation systems
   d. insufficient supplies of wood

7. The middle-class housewife was to
   a. work outside of the home to help support the family's lifestyle.
   b. exhibit independence and reject traditional values of womanhood.
   c. avoid any involvement in social reforms.
   d. keep the home functioning properly and serve as a model for moral purity.

8. During the second half of the nineteenth century, all of the following countries challenged British industrial supremacy except _____.
   a. Austria
   b. the United States
   c. Germany
   d. France

9. The Great Famine of 1845–1851 occurred in _____.
   a. England
   b. Russia
   c. France
   d. Ireland

10. In the factory system
    a. all workers operated according to the discipline of the whistle.
    b. workers found themselves stripped of guild protections.
    c. the manufacturing process was broken down into specialized tasks.
    d. all of the above

11. Middle-class homes
    a. were built to last a long time.
    b. stood as symbols of material and social status.
    c. were often crowded with furniture and art.
    d. all of the above

12. Working women and children in England
    a. represented almost half of the labor force in the textile industry.
    b. rarely worked in dangerous jobs.
    c. were paid remarkably low wages.
    d. both a and c

MATCHING

1. Factory Acts
2. Thomas Newcomen
3. navvies
4. water frame
5. John Kay
6. Samuel Compton
7. Edward Jenner
8. Eli Whitney
9. James Hargreaves
10. George Stephenson

a. invented the spinning mule
b. cloth spinning machine
c. created a vaccine for smallpox
d. designed the first steam railway
e. invented the spinning jenny
f. railway workers
g. limited working hours for children
h. invented the flying shuttle
i. invented the cotton gin
j. his steam engine pumped water from mines

TRUE/FALSE

1. Commercialized agriculture was an important root cause of industrialization in Britain.

2. British aristocrats refused to participate in business activities and instead lived off of inherited wealth.

3. Britain refused to export coal to prevent continental Europe from industrializing.

4. England's first railroad line ran from London to Manchester.

5. In eastern Europe, commercialized agriculture created huge food surpluses for export.

6. Limited liability laws enabled shareholders to avoid liability for a company's debts.

7. According to the text, the initial phase of the industrial revolution largely was restricted to industries that made cheaper clothes, better metals, and faster travel.

8. Governments legalized prostitution as an outlet for males.

9. Respectable middle-class men shunned aristocratic behavior.

10. According to the text, air pollution played little role in deaths attributed to bronchitis and tuberculosis.

PUT THE FOLLOWING ITEMS IN CHRONOLOGICAL ORDER

1. Invention of Watt's steam engine   _____

2. Invention of the flying shuttle   _____

3. Invention of Stephenson's railway   _____

4. Invention of the cotton gin   _____

5. Invention of Newcomen's steam engine   _____

6. Invention of the spinning mule   _____

7. Invention of the spinning jenny   _____

SHORT ANSWER AND ESSAY QUESTIONS

A. The Industrial Revolution in Britain

1. Why did the Industrial Revolution begin in Britain?
2. Trace the steps of industrialization in cotton manufacturing.
3. What developments occurred in the iron industry?
4. Explain the importance of the steam engine and the development of railroads.
5. Consider how steam engines, textile machines, the iron industry, and the railroads are all interconnected.

B. The Industrial Revolution after 1850 and on the Continent

1. Why did changes in Britain not appear on the Continent until after 1830?
2. In what ways was the Industrial Revolution on the Continent different from the developments in Britain?
3. What were the major changes in the Industrial Revolution during the second half of the nineteenth century? Which countries took the lead?
4. What were the economic patterns of development in eastern Europe in the nineteenth century?
5. How were various empires linked to trade?

C. The social consequences of industrialization

1. What are the various explanations for the population explosion in the nineteenth century? Which is now considered the most likely explanation?
2. Compare the letters in the selection "The Irish Famine: Interpretations and Responses." How do these letters show the changing social assumptions? Which is closest in view to Malthus? Explain why you made that judgment.

D. The urban landscape

1. Describe life in the cities in the early nineteenth century for the working class.
2. Describe the various groups within the middle class.
3. How were members of the middle class able to rise in society?
4. How did members of the middle class view themselves? What did they see as the correct behavior?
5. In theory, what were the responsibilities of a middle-class wife? What did it take to run a household?
6. Compare working-class and middle-class attitudes toward sex and sexuality. How do the selections in "Marriage, Sexuality, and the Facts of Life" apply to this comparison?

E. Middle-class and working-class lives

1. What was the public life of the nineteenth-century middle class?
2. Describe the various groups within the working class.
3. Describe the life of working women. How did middle-class writers perceive the life of working women? How did this compare with the actual life of working women?
4. What were the new problems faced by the working class in the cities during the Industrial Revolution?

F. Overview

1. Why was the Industrial Revolution one of the turning points in the history of the world?
2. Write an essay on how industrialization created new forms of wealth alongside new kinds of poverty.

MULTIPLE CHOICE KEY

1. d
2. b
3. c
4. c
5. c
6. d
7. d
8. a
9. d
10. d
11. d
12. d

MATCHING KEY

1. g
2. j
3. f
4. b
5. h
6. a
7. c
8. i
9. e
10. d

TRUE/FALSE KEY

1. T
2. F
3. F
4. F
5. T
6. T
7. T
8. T
9. T
10. F

CHRONOLOGICAL ORDER KEY

5, 1, 7, 2, 4, 6, 3

CHAPTER 20

From Restoration to Revolution, 1815–1848

In many ways, the first half of the nineteenth century was a reaction to the French Revolution and the Napoleonic era. This chapter discusses that reaction first in terms of politics, as related to events and new political ideas and theories, and secondly in terms of cultural developments. Then it returns to the political events of the mid-century, incorporating some of the new political perspectives in opposition to old perspectives and the resulting conflicts.

CHAPTER OUTLINE

1. Introduction

2. Back to the future: Restoring order, 1815–1830
   a. The Congress of Vienna and the Restoration
   b. Revolt against Restoration
   c. Revolution in Latin America
   d. Russia: the Decembrists
   e. Southeastern Europe: Greece and Serbia

3. Taking sides: new ideologies in politics
   a. Principles of conservatism
   b. Liberalism
   c. Radicalism, republicanism, and early socialism
   d. Karl Marx's socialism
   e. Citizenship and community: nationalism

4. Cultural revolt: Romanticism
   a. British romantic poetry
   b. Women writers, gender, and Romanticism
   c. Romantic painting
   d. Romantic politics: liberty, history, and nation
   e. Orientalism
   f. Goethe and Beethoven

5. Reform and revolution
   a. The 1830 revolution in France
   b. Belgium and Poland in 1830
   c. Reform in Great Britain
   d. British radicalism and the Chartist movement
   e. "The Hungry Forties" and the revolutions of 1848
   f. The French revolution of 1848

6. Conclusion

IDENTIFY

1. Klemens von Metternich
2. Congress of Vienna
3. Chartist movement
4. Louis Philippe
5. Carbonari
6. Decembrists
7. Greek war for independence
8. conservatism
9. liberalism
10. socialism
11. Karl Marx
12. nationalism
13. Romanticism
14. Orientalism
15. Goethe

MULTIPLE CHOICE

1. Metternich's primary objectives at the Congress of Vienna involved
   a. thwarting Russian territorial expansion into Europe.
   b. codifying the liberal gains of the French Revolution.
   c. preventing political and social change.
   d. both a and c

2. The great powers created an arrangement at the Congress of Vienna
   a. in which none of them received territory out of a conviction that such acquisitions might create diplomatic friction.
   b. that prevented successful revolutions from occurring in Europe.
   c. that enabled Europe to avoid a general war for about a century.
   d. all of the above

3. Tsar Nicholas I reacted to the insurrection of the Decembrists by
   a. executing the leaders and imprisoning mutinous soldiers.
   b. abolishing serfdom and freeing the nobility from state service.
   c. appealing to Metternich to send troops to crush the rebellion.
   d. giving in to most of their demands for reform while maintaining the institution of serfdom.

4. Europeans supported the Greeks in their war for independence because
   a. of a desire to prevent Russia from gaining access to the Mediterranean.
   b. the rebellion was framed as a religious conflict.
   c. of the importance of Greece to Western civilization.
   d. both b and c

5. Conservatives essentially held the view that
   a. the monarchy provided a country with political stability.
   b. nobles benefited countries by providing leaders.
   c. slow, piecemeal change that strengthened the natural order of society is acceptable.
   d. all of the above

6. Nineteenth-century liberals would most likely favor all of the following except _____.
   a. extending voting rights
   b. economic equality
   c. equality before the law
   d. representative government

7. Which of the following statements about Karl Marx is incorrect?
   a. He saw history as passing through stages shaped by conflict among social groups.
   b. His deeply held religious views shaped his commitment to economic equality.
   c. He wrote the *Communist Manifesto*.
   d. He believed that capitalism would ultimately succumb to recurring economic crises.

8. Which one of the following is not a Romantic poet?
   a. Wordsworth
   b. Turner
   c. Coleridge
   d. Keats

9. Lord Byron's "romantic" impulses led him to
   a. rebel against political and social conventions.
   b. defend the interests of the working class.
   c. support the Greeks in their war for independence.
   d. all of the above

10. Perhaps the major event that triggered Europe's interest in the Orient was
    a. the Greek war for independence against the Turks.
    b. Napoleon's invasion of Egypt.
    c. the publication of Lord Byron's first book of poems.
    d. the 1848 revolution in France.

11. The Reform Bill of 1832
    a. increased parliamentary representation in the industrial north.
    b. increased the number of eligible voters.
    c. destroyed the Whigs politically.
    d. both a and b

12. The National Workshops in France
    a. were political "banquets" held to rally forces to the cause of socialism.
    b. employed workers for public works projects in and around Paris.
    c. surprisingly added needed funds to the French treasury.
    d. both b and c

MATCHING

1. Metternich	a. pledged to cooperate against insurrections
2. Alexander I	
3. Concert of Europe	b. promoted free markets
4. Carbonari	c. overthrown in 1830
5. Bolívar	d author of *Frankenstein*
6. Turner	e. architect of the Congress of Vienna
7. Burke	
8. Blanc	f. advocated government workshops
9. Smith	
10. Shelley	g. Italian opposition to the conservative order
11. Chartists	
12. Charles X	h. sought universal manhood suffrage
	i. regarded "natural rights" as dangerous
	j. Romantic painter
	k. declared a Holy Alliance
	l. Latin American revolutionary

TRUE/FALSE

1. At Vienna, Metternich treated France leniently because of his concerns about Russian ambitions in Europe.

2. After the Congress of Vienna, the great powers of Europe justified their conception of "legitimacy" as sanctioned by God.

3. Shortly before the Greek victory over the Ottomans, Serbia became completely independent from the Ottoman Empire.

4. All liberals were strong supporters of universal manhood suffrage but were reluctant to extend universal voting rights to women.

5. Laissez-faire economics calls upon governments to regulate the economy.

6. Workers in New Lanark benefited from entrepreneur Robert Owen's genuine concern for their welfare.

7. Romantic artists championed individualism and elevated emotion and imagination over reason.

8. Goethe's *Faust* recounts the tale of a man who sold his soul to the devil.

9. Opposition to the reign of Louis Philippe pushed for electoral reform.

10. Louis Napoleon's reforms made France a republic.

PUT THE FOLLOWING ITEMS IN CHRONOLOGICAL ORDER

1. Decembrist uprising   _____

2. Greece became independent   _____

3. The Congress of Vienna   _____

4. June Days   _____

5. Louis Napoleon crowned emperor _____

SHORT ANSWER AND ESSAY QUESTIONS

A. Restoring order

1. What were the guiding principles of the Congress of Vienna?
2. What were the stipulations of the treaty written at the Congress of Vienna? Did these stipulations match the original goals and principles?
3. What was the "Concert of Europe"? How did it function and what was its purpose?

B. Revolt against restoration

1. How had events in Europe during the Napoleonic era changed the political situation in Latin America?
2. What were the various reasons behind the revolt of the Decembrists?
3. Why did the Greek war for independence capture so much attention from other European states? How was this expressed?

C. New ideologies in politics

1. What was the basis of early nineteenth-century conservatism? How were Edmund Burke's ideas from *Reflections on a Revolution in France* incorporated into this view?
2. What did liberalism mean during the nineteenth century? What were the goals of nineteenth-century liberalism?
3. What is economic liberalism?
4. What were the views and goals of socialism?
5. What was Marx's theory of history? How did he apply it to his political theory?
6. Compare and contrast the ideologies of nineteenth-century conservatism, liberalism, socialism, and communism. Draw a chart that reflects the economic and political approach of conservatism, liberalism, and socialism during the nineteenth century.
7. How did the meaning of "nation" change over time? How did conservatives and liberals differ in their interpretation of "nationalism"?
8. What were the principal political ideologies of the early nineteenth century?

D. Romanticism

1. What were the characteristics of Romanticism? Using the works of various writers and artists as examples, illustrate the basic themes of Romanticism.
2. In what ways did the story *Frankenstein* reflect Romantic views?
3. Explain how nationalism was linked to Romanticism by both liberals and conservatives.
4. What was the perception of the "East" or Orient held by western Europeans? Why did it develop during this period?
5. What were the contributions of Goethe and Beethoven?

E. Reform and revolution

1. What were the political ideologies of the revolutionaries in France, Belgium, and Poland in 1830? What was the outcome in each case?
2. How was the 1830 revolution in France a repudiation of the actions of Charles X? What are some of the reasons for unrest as put forth in the selection of "Popular Unrest in Paris, 1828"?
3. What led to the British Reform Bill of 1832? What did it accomplish?
4. What were the six demands in the People's Charter? What was the goal of Chartism in England? By what means did the Chartists try to obtain their goal?
5. Trace the three changes in government in France in 1848. Explain not only what changed but also the reasons why.

6. Compare the "Two Views of the June Days, France, 1848." What does each tell about the June Days? What are the political views of Marx and Tocqueville? What is the significance of the June Days?
7. How did Louis Napoleon consolidate his power?

F. Overall

1. Discuss Romanticism's impact on literature and art. How did Romanticism reflect the political ideals of the nineteenth century?

MULTIPLE CHOICE KEY

1. d
2. c
3. a
4. d
5. d
6. b
7. b
8. b
9. d
10. b
11. d
12. b

MATCHING KEY

1. e
2. k
3. a
4. g
5. l
6. j
7. i
8. f
9. b
10. d
11. h
12. c

TRUE/FALSE KEY

1. T
2. F
3. F
4. F
5. F
6. T
7. T
8. T
9. T
10. F

CHRONOLOGICAL ORDER KEY

3, 1, 2, 4, 5

CHAPTER 21

What Is a Nation? Territories, States, and Citizens, 1848–1871

This chapter focuses on a number of political changes between 1848 and 1871. Many of these changes reflected a desire to establish or strengthen national states. This was part of a movement known as "nationalism" referred to in the last chapter. For nation-states, economic development and political transformation became a means of securing the state's power.

CHAPTER OUTLINE

1. Introduction

2. Nationalism and revolution in 1848
   a. What makes a nation? Germany in 1848
   b. The Frankfurt Assembly and German nationhood
   c. Peoples against empire: the Habsburg lands
   d. 1848 in Austria and Hungary: springtime of peoples and the autumn of empire
   e. 1848 and the early states of Italian unification

3. Building the nation-state
   a. France under Napoleon III
   b. Victorian England and the Second Reform Bill (1867)
   c. Italian unification: Cavour and Garibaldi
   d. The unification of Germany: Realpolitik
   e. The state and nationality: centrifugal forces in the Austrian empire

4. Nation and state building in Russia, the United States, and Canada
   a. Territory, the state, and serfdom: Russia
   b. Territory, the nation-state, and slavery: the United States
   c. Territorial expansion: Canada

   d. Eastern questions and international relations
      i. The Crimean War, 1854–1856
   e. Realism: "Democracy in Art"

5. Conclusion

IDENTIFY

1. Zollverein
2. Frankfurt Assembly
3. Lajos Kossuth
4. Giuseppe Mazzini
5. Napoleon III
6. Benjamin Disraeli
7. John Stuart Mill
8. Count Cavour
9. Giuseppe Garibaldi
10. Otto von Bismarck
11. Franco-Prussian War
12. Dual Monarchy
13. Jeffersonian Revolution
14. Crimean War
15. realism

MULTIPLE CHOICE

1. All of the following events occurred in 1848 except _____.
   a. the Seneca Falls Convention
   b. the Frankfurt Assembly
   c. the abolition of serfdom in Russia
   d. the Treaty of Guadalupe Hidalgo

2. The main goal of the Frankfurt Assembly was to
   a. enlist the Prussian army in a war against Austria.
   b. create a German nation-state.
   c. draft a liberal constitution for a renewed Holy Roman empire.
   d. prevent the revolution in France from spreading to the German states.

3. The leader of Hungary's independence movement in 1848–1849 was _____.
   a. Frantis ek Palacky
   b. Jan Kollár
   c. Adam Mickiewicz
   d. none of the above

4. The initial response of the Austrian government to the revolution in 1848 was to
   a. use troops to disband the Hungarian Diet.
   b. acquiesce and agree to reform the government.
   c. unleash Metternich and his political spies on student demonstrators in Vienna.
   d. crush the insurgency wherever it appeared.

5. Mazzini's Young Italy
   a. wanted to remove Austria from northern Italy and create a unified Italian nation-state.
   b. ultimately collapsed when Pope Gregory XVI withdrew his support of the organization.
   c. succeeded in conquering Sardinia but failed to inspire Italian nationalism.
   d. both a and b

6. All of the following are correct regarding Napoleon III's France except
   a. workers gained the right to organize and strike.
   b. the emperor conducted his own foreign policy and controlled the army and government finances.
   c. Napoleon III undertook an aggressive and overwhelmingly successful foreign policy.
   d. he encouraged economic development through the use of credit, free trade, and limited liability laws.

7. Benjamin Disraeli supported the Reform Bill of 1867 because he
   a. was a strong advocate of voting rights for men and women.
   b. thought newly enfranchised workers would support the Conservative party.
   c. thought it could prevent the outbreak of a socialist revolution.
   d. none of the above

8. Count Cavour prevented Garibaldi from "liberating" Rome
   a. because he feared France or Austria might intervene.
   b. he wanted to unite Italy under Piedmont-Sardinia's leadership.
   c. under an alliance with the pope that granted the pontiff control of the papal states.
   d. both a and b

9. Bismarck created a unified German nation
   a. following wars against Denmark, Austria, and France.
   b. because he believed it was his duty as a German and a statesman.
   c. that essentially imposed Prussian domination on smaller German states.
   d. both a and c

10. The Franco-Prussian War began after
    a. Bismarck carefully edited a telegram regarding a meeting between the Prussian king and a French diplomat.
    b. Bismarck insulted Napoleon III at Versailles.
    c. France invaded the Rhineland.
    d. Austria and France formed an anti-Prussian alliance.

11. According to the federal structure of the Dual Monarchy,
    a. Hungary controlled its own military and foreign affairs, but had its domestic policy directed by the Austrian emperor.
    b. Hungary and Austria shared a common army and cooperated on foreign and military policies.
    c. Bohemia created its own constitution and legislature but remained allied to Austria-Hungary.
    d. Budapest became the capital of the Austrian empire.

12. All of the following are correct regarding the abolition of serfdom in Russia except
    a. some 22 million serfs gained legal rights.
    b. land granted to ex-serfs was actually given to a village commune.
    c. the land granted to ex-serfs was among the most fertile in Russia.
    d. big landowners managed to keep their most productive lands.

MATCHING

1. Zollverein
2. Lajos Kossuth
3. Franz Joseph
4. Crédit Mobilier
5. Baron Haussmann
6. "The Thousand"
7. Bismarck
8. Franco-Prussian War
9. Alexander II
10. Zola

a. presided over the rebuilding of Paris
b. the architect of German unification
c. ended Napoleon III's reign
d. free trade zone
e. examined urban social problems
f. Hungarian nationalist leader
g. French investment bank
h. freed the serfs
i. Garibaldi's fighters
j. emperor of Austria

TRUE/FALSE

1. Nationalism is generally regarded as an ideology that supported liberal goals in the early nineteenth century and conservative goals in the latter half of the century.

2. The German Confederation was a loose association of German states excluding Austria.

3. Austria was the dominant economic power in the Zollverein.

4. A major problem for the Austrian monarchy in the nineteenth century was the increasing nationalism of its numerous minorities.

5. In 1848, the papacy allied with Garibaldi to expel the French from the Papal states.

6. In *The Subjection of Women*, Mill connected women's liberation with social progress.

7. To drive the Austrians out of Italy, Cavour entered into an alliance with Russia.

8. The "slavophiles" thought Russian greatness necessitated the adoption of European advances in science, technology, and education.

9. While making Canada independent, the 1867 Act of Parliament also gave it dominion status within the British Commonwealth.

10. Immediately following the Crimean War, Russia gained additional influence in the Balkans.

PUT THE FOLLOWING ITEMS IN CHRONOLOGICAL ORDER

1. The Seven Weeks' War   _____

2. The Frankfurt Assembly   _____

3. The Franco-Prussian War   _____

4. The emancipation of Russian serfs   _____

5. The Crimean War   _____

SHORT ANSWER AND ESSAY QUESTIONS

A. Nationalism

1. What measures did Prussians take to establish their dominance within the German Confederation?

2. What problems confronted the Frankfurt Assembly as it attempted to form a unified liberal German State?

3. Using the selection "Frederick William IV Refuses the 'Throne from the Gutter,'" explain why Frederick William IV refused to become ruler of the German nation in 1849.

4. What ethnic groups were there within the Habsburg empire? Why was this a problem for the rulers of Austria?

5. What was pan-Slavism? How did it change after 1848?

6. What measures did the Habsburgs take in 1848 and 1849 to counteract revolts in various areas of the empire?

7. What were the various divisions of political states in the Italian peninsula in 1848? How was each ruled?

B. France under Napoleon III

1. In what ways did France modernize under Napoleon III?

C. Victorian England

1. Why were members of the working class in Britain less interested in militant radicalism? What did they establish instead?

2. Explain the reasons various groups backed the Reform Bill of 1867. What were the results of the Bill?

3. Explain the ideas found in John Stuart Mill's *On Liberty*. Why was this so significant in defining the ideas of Western liberalism?

D. Italian unification

1. Compare the approaches of Cavour and Garibaldi toward Italian unification. Explain the goals of each and how they each intended to achieve unification.

2. Trace the steps taken toward unification and consolidation of the Italian states.

E. German confederation

1. Define *Realpolitik*. Why was Bismarck such a good example of its practice?

2. What occurred at the various stages of German unification?

3. How was the German empire formed?

4. What problems weakened the Habsburgs within their empire? How did Francis Joseph deal with these?

F. Nation and state building elsewhere

1. What were the similarities between slavery and serfdom?

2. Compare the two views on serfdom in "The Abolition of Serfdom in Russia." What did Alexander II expect? What problems did the serfs point out in their petitions?

3. What were the political, economic, and ethical implications of the territorial expansion of the United States?

4. What were the results of the American Civil War?

5. How did Canadian expansion differ from that in the United States? How was the process similar?

G. Crimean War

1. What led to the Crimean War? What were the geographic implications for states in the area?
2. Explain the reasons why each state involved in the Crimean War participated.
3. What were the results of the Crimean War?

H. Realism

1. What does the term *realism* mean in art?

I. Overall

1. How did statesmen consolidate power and build nations from above?
2. What forms did nationalism take in different countries?

MULTIPLE CHOICE KEY

1. c
2. b
3. d
4. b
5. a
6. c
7. b
8. d
9. d
10. a
11. b
12. c

MATCHING KEY

1. d
2. f
3. j
4. g
5. a
6. i
7. b
8. c
9. h
10. e

TRUE/FALSE KEY

1. T
2. F
3. F
4. T
5. F
6. T
7. F
8. F
9. T
10. F

CHRONOLOGICAL ORDER KEY

2, 5, 4, 1, 3

CHAPTER 22 | Imperialism and Colonialism, 1870–1914

This chapter covers what was known as the "new imperialism" in the period between 1870 and 1914. It looks at the rapid extension of European control in other areas of the world. It discusses how technology, money, and politics merged to create empires in the late nineteenth century. The chapter explores how developments discussed in previous chapters, such as industrialization, revolution, and the rise of nation-states, changed the nature of imperialism and created a new "self-conscious imperial" culture.

CHAPTER OUTLINE

1. Introduction

2. Imperialism

3. Imperialism in South Asia
   a. "The mutiny"

4. Imperialism in China
   a. The opium trade
   b. The Boxer Rebellion
   c. Russian imperialism

5. The French empire and the civilizing mission

6. The "scramble for Africa" and the Congo
   a. The Congo Free State
   b. The partition of Africa

7. Imperial culture
   a. Colonial culture

8. Crises of empire at the turn of the twentieth century
   a. Fashoda
   b. South Africa: the Boer War
   c. U.S. imperialism

9. Conclusion

IDENTIFY

1. new imperialism
2. British East India Company
3. Sepoy Rebellion
4. Boer War
5. Russian imperialism
6. The Taipin Rebellion
7. The Boxer Rebellion
8. Jules Ferry
9. King Leopold II
10. Herero
11. Cecil Rhodes
12. Splendid Little War
13. Count Arthur de Gobineau
14. Houston Stewart Chamberlain
15. Fashoda

MULTIPLE CHOICE

1. The British government intervened in Egyptian affairs in 1882
   a. to prevent the Ottomans from reestablishing control in Egypt.
   b. to prevent the French from incorporating Egypt into their North African empire.
   c. to protect their investments and to control the government.
   d. as a way of diverting attention from an unpleasant domestic crisis.

2. The opening of ports in China with special trading privileges for Europeans is an example of _____.
   a. informal imperialism
   b. formal imperialism

c. colonialism

d. both b and c

3. The "scramble for Africa" occurred

   a. in the early nineteenth century when Britain and France vied for control of Egypt.

   b. essentially during the last two decades of the nineteenth century.

   c. around the time of the Opium Wars, when England looked for new areas to grow poppies.

   d. immediately following the Boer War.

4. Which of the following is incorrect regarding the British East India Company in the first half of the nineteenth century?

   a. It had its own military.

   b. It had the right to collect taxes.

   c. It had a monopoly only on the opium trade.

   d. It governed some parts of India directly and other parts indirectly.

5. The British response following the end of "the mutiny" was to

   a. give the British East India Company a greater role in governing India.

   b. eliminate the use of native troops in the military.

   c. abolish the British East India Company.

   d. increase missionary activity to turn Indians into Christian pacifists.

6. As a result of the 1842 Treaty of Nanking

   a. Britain acquired additional trading privileges in China and the port of Hong Kong.

   b. the Chinese were able to reduce the importation of opium.

   c. Britain appointed a viceroy to govern China.

   d. both a and c

7. Russia and Britain almost went to war

   a. over competing interests in the Middle East.

   b. when Russia demanded to be included in the "scramble for Africa."

   c. after Russia supplied the Boers with weapons.

   d. during Russia's expansion into the Kurile Islands.

8. The Federation of French West Africa

   a. governed an area larger than France.

   b. made efforts to improve sanitation, healthcare, and water systems.

   c. created a constitution that gave political rights to both African elites and peasants.

   d. both a and b

9. According to Count Arthur de Gobineau, what was the key to understanding problems of the modern world?

   a. social class

   b. race

   c. gender

   d. economics

10. All of the following are results of European colonial ventures except

   a. new hybrid cultures emerged through European contact with indigenous peoples.

   b. European labor demands created a highly disciplined labor force.

   c. European and native elites questioned the impact of westernization.

   d. European administrators worried about the impact of sexual relations between European men and indigenous women.

11. The incident at Fashoda

   a. involved British attempts to corner the diamond market in southern Africa.

   b. saw the British general Horatio Kitchener massacre the Mahdi's army.

   c. became a national scandal for England over their use of concentration camps.

   d. nearly resulted in a war between France and Britain.

12. During the Boer War

   a. Europeans fought European settlers.

   b. the British instituted concentration camps.

   c. Afrikaners used guerrilla tactics.

   d. all of the above

MATCHING

1. Suez Canal	a. the Sepoy Rebellion
2. Omdurman	b. European settlers in South Africa
3. formal imperialism	c. nearly annihilated by the Germans
4. "the mutiny"	
5. India	d. connected the Mediterranean and Red Seas
6. W. E. B. Du Bois	
7. Herrero	e. founded DeBeers
8. Cecil Rhodes	f. colonialism
9. Francis Galton	g. the jewel of the British crown
10. Afrikaners	h. promoted eugenics
	i. British victory in the Sudan
	j. identified the problem of the color line

TRUE/FALSE

1. Imperialism involves the extension of one country's control over another country.

2. By 1902, Europeans had colonized around 90 percent of the African continent.

3. Russian imperialism focused exclusively on eastern Europe.

4. One of the benefits of colonial markets was that people there were able to purchase much of the surplus manufacturing in Europe.

5. "The mutiny" occurred after a group of Indian soldiers refused to use rifle cartridges moistened with cow blood.

6. The Transvaal and Orange Free State were Afrikaner republics.

7. Algeria was France's most significant settler colony.

8. The British women's suffrage movement emerged out of various anti-imperialist societies.

9. Delegates at the London Pan-African Conference of 1900 used late-nineteenth-century racial science to justify imperialism.

10. After defeating Spain, the United States annexed Puerto Rico and established a protectorate over Cuba.

PUT THE FOLLOWING ITEMS IN CHRONOLOGICAL ORDER

1. Opening of the Suez Canal _____

2. Boxer Rebellion _____

3. Confrontation at Fashoda _____

4. "The mutiny" _____

5. Treaty of Nanking _____

SHORT ANSWER AND ESSAY QUESTIONS

A. Imperialism

1. What is imperialism?
2. What were the causes of the "new imperialism"?
3. How did industrialization change the nature of imperialism? How did the rise of nation-states change the nature of imperialism?

B. British India

1. How was the British East India Company organized and how did it function?
2. Why was formal, direct rule of India taken over by the British government in 1861?
3. What was the catalyst for the Sepoy Rebellion? What were the real causes?
4. What changes in India did the British make after "the mutiny"?

C. Imperialism in China

1. How did European imperialism develop in China? How did this differ from other areas where imperialism existed?
2. Why were European powers anxious to establish treaty ports and spheres of influence in China?
3. Why was control of Chinese markets particularly crucial to British economic interests?
4. Explain the core issues between the imperial powers and China. How did these issues turn violent at various times?

D. Russian and French pursuits

1. Study a map and examine the territory the Russians added during the nineteenth century. Why do you think they expanded into these areas?
2. Explain the various ways in which France's Algeria was unique among the territories under European control? How did policies enacted there differ from other imperial colonies?
3. What was the concept of the French "civilizing mission"? How and where was this pursued?

E. Africa

1. What was the plight of the people in the Congo described in George Washington Williams' letter in the selection "Atrocities in the Congo"? What was the reaction of the Europeans to this situation? How was it resolved?
2. Compare the maps of Africa in 1886 and 1914. Which European states controlled the most territory? Which controlled the least?
3. How did the "scramble for Africa" unfold on the African continent?

F. Imperial culture

1. Compare the two selections under "Rudyard Kipling and His Critics." How did Kipling regard the endeavor of ruling an empire? What did he think was entailed? How was this challenged in the reply?
2. How did empire affect Europeans' identity of themselves?

G. Crises of empire

1. What were the circumstances regarding the situation at Fashoda in 1898?
2. Why was the Boer War such a turning point in the British empire?
3. What brought the United States into war against Spain in 1898? How did this change America's approach to empire?

MULTIPLE CHOICE KEY

1. c
2. a
3. b
4. c
5. c
6. a
7. a
8. d
9. b
10. b
11. d
12. d

MATCHING KEY

1. d
2. i
3. f
4. a
5. g
6. j
7. c
8. e
9. h
10. b

TRUE/FALSE KEY

1. T
2. T
3. F
4. F
5. F
6. T
7. T
8. F
9. F
10. T

CHRONOLOGICAL ORDER KEY

5, 4, 1, 3, 2

CHAPTER 23 | Modern Industry and Mass Politics, 1870–1914

The chapter's theme discusses changes occurring between 1870 and 1914, which resulted in a number of new challenges for Europe and the world. These changes came from a number of different areas and affected groups, individuals, and governments. Mass consumption and mass politics became part of life, and new groups became involved in the political process. The "second industrial revolution" drastically altered European life. The intellectual and cultural atmosphere was such that, by 1914, Europeans had questioned all previously established values and assumptions.

CHAPTER OUTLINE

1. Introduction

2. New technologies and global transformations
   a. Challenges in scope and scale
   b. The rise of the corporation
   c. International economics

3. Labor, politics, and mass movements
   a. The spread of socialist parties—and alternatives
   b. The limits of success

4. Demanding equality: suffrage and the women's movement
   a. Redefining womanhood

5. Liberalism and its discontents: national politics at the turn of the century
   a. France: the embattled republic
   b. The Dreyfus Affair and anti-Semitism as politics
   c. Zionism
   d. Germany's search for imperial unity

   e. Britain: from moderation to militance
   f. Russia: the road to revolution
      i. The first Russian revolution
   g. Nationalism and imperial politics: the Balkans

6. The science and soul of the modern age
   a. Darwin's revolutionary theory
      i. Darwinian theory and religion
   b. Social Darwinism
   c. Early psychology: Pavlov and Freud
   d. Nietzsche's attack on tradition
   e. New readers and the popular press
   f. The first moderns: innovations in art
      i. The revolt on canvas

7. Conclusion

IDENTIFY

1. second industrial revolution
2. *Capital*
3. anarchism
4. Emmeline Pankhurst
5. Paris Commune
6. Dreyfus Affair
7. Theodore Herzl
8. French Impressionists
9. German Social Democrats
10. Sigmund Freud
11. Social Darwinism
12. Populists
13. Vladimir Lenin
14. October Manifesto
15. Young Turks

MULTIPLE CHOICE

1. The second industrial revolution centered on all of the following technologies except _____.
   a. electricity
   b. iron
   c. steel
   d. chemicals

2. The population of Europe increased and the general health of the people improved because of
   a. better crop yields and the ability to ship food long distances.
   b. advances in medicine, nutrition, and personal hygiene.
   c. better housing and public sanitation.
   d. all of the above

3. Which of the following is incorrect regarding Marx and Marxism?
   a. Marxists were among the forefront in arguing for the expansion of civil liberties, including the right to vote.
   b. Marxists supported gender equality but the issue was never as significant as class politics.
   c. All working-class movements were Marxist and committed to overthrowing the capitalist system through revolution.
   d. Marx's *Capital* served as the most prominent critique of capitalism.

4. The Women's Social and Political Union
   a. engaged in a militant campaign to gain voting rights for women.
   b. was led by Millicent Fawcett.
   c. enjoyed considerable support in Parliament for their moderate tactics.
   d. was a largely conventional social club that instructed middle-class women in Victorian virtues.

5. The French government's response to the Commune in Paris was to
   a. supply it with weapons to continue the war against Germany.
   b. accept most of its demands concerning the creation of the Third Republic.
   c. send troops to Paris to crush the communards.
   d. negotiate with its leaders until the Commune surrendered.

6. The Dreyfus Affair
   a. revealed the considerable degree of anti-Semitism in France.
   b. caused the Catholic Church to call for the removal of all anti-Semites in the French high command.
   c. ultimately led to the separation of church and state in France.
   d. both a and c

7. The political structure of the German empire established by Bismarck
   a. included a two-house legislature that chose the emperor.
   b. required the emperor to seek Reichstag approval before appointing cabinet members.
   c. protected the privileges of German elites and ensured a dominant political role for Prussia.
   d. unified Germany politically and socially.

8. Bismarck responded to the spread of socialism in Germany by
   a. supporting antisocialist laws and attacking the Social Democrats.
   b. supporting social welfare legislation for German workers.
   c. ignoring the Social Democrats because it was a minority party.
   d. both a and b

9. Revolution in Russia occurred in 1905
   a. because of an unsuccessful war against Japan.
   b. because of successful agitation by the Bolsheviks and Mensheviks.
   c. after the Duma finally decided to assert its authority over Russia's foreign policy.
   d. both a and c

10. In the Ottoman Empire, the Young Turks
    a. compelled the sultan to establish a constitutional government.
    b. gave greater freedoms to non-Turkish inhabitants of the Ottoman Empire.
    c. attempted to "Ottomanize" the empire by extending Turkish culture and restricting the rights of non-Turks.
    d. both a and c

11. Religious leaders were particularly disturbed by Darwin's theory of evolution because
    a. Darwin denied the existence of God and declared the Bible to be a complete work of fiction.
    b. in the *Origin of Species*, Darwin was able to prove how man came from a monkey.
    c. the theory challenged the idea of a benevolent god and a morally guided universe governed by divine will.
    d. both b and c

12. The work of both Sigmund Freud and Ivan Pavlov supported the notion that
    a. human behavior was guided by genetics and could be altered only by medicine.
    b. unconscious and irrational forces guided human behavior.
    c. human reason was the principal cause of behavior but humans nevertheless acted irrationally.
    d. the culture, morals, and values of a society should be stressed as a way to prevent irrational behavior.

MATCHING

1. Harold Lever
2. Thomas Edison
3. Theodore Herzl
4. home rule
5. Zemstvos
6. Populists
7. October Manifesto
8. Ottoman Empire
9. Herbert Spencer
10. Claude Monet

a. advocated Social Darwinism
b. painted the interaction of light on surfaces
c. soap pioneer
d. Russian provincial assemblies
e. radical Russian political group
f. self-government for Ireland
g. the sick man of Europe
h. invented the incandescent–filament lamp
i. guaranteed individual liberties
j. championed Zionism

TRUE/FALSE

1. Prior to World War I, Germany controlled about 90 percent of the world's chemical market.

2. Limited liability laws protected stockholders when corporations went bankrupt.

3. Anarchists adopted peaceful tactics to promote democratic reforms.

4. The Mensheviks' call for immediate revolution alienated the Bolsheviks.

5. The advance of democracy slowed the development of socialist parties.

6. The largest political party in Germany on the eve of World War I was the Social Democratic party.

7. Syndicalists supported the use of strikes and sabotage to achieve their goals.

8. Father Gapon led the "Bloody Sunday" uprising.

9. Yellow journalism is characterized by an emphasis on hard news stories rather than sensationalism.

10. Nietzsche advocated a search for truth beginning with a thorough grounding in scripture and the latest scientific advancements.

PUT THE FOLLOWING ITEMS IN CHRONOLOGICAL ORDER

1. October Manifesto issued _____

2. Assassination of Alexander II _____

3. Publication of *Capital* _____

4. Publication of *Origin of Species* _____

5. Young Turks depose the sultan _____

SHORT ANSWER AND ESSAY QUESTIONS

A. New technologies and global transformations

1. What were the three major technological advances of the second industrial revolution? Explain how and why they made such a great impact.
2. What was the change in patterns of consumption?

B. Economics

1. How did modern corporations organize to compete internationally? What did the corporations see as advantages of these kinds of organizations? What were the disadvantages of them?
2. How did large companies finance and organize their businesses? How did this differ from earlier methods?
3. Discuss the implications of the growth of international competition of businesses.

C. Labor politics, mass movements

1. Discuss the changes to labor unions that occurred in the second half of the nineteenth century. What were the reasons behind these changes?
2. Discuss the different working class political movements, particularly the various interpretations of socialism. Explain their appeal.
3. Compare the goals of the German Social Democratic party and the British Labour party. Why did they differ?

D. Demanding equality

1. What legal reforms were made for women at the turn of the century?
2. How did the employment of women change at the end of the nineteenth century? What were the reasons behind these changes?
3. What were the characteristics of the "new woman"?

E. National politics

1. How did the Paris Commune affect the long-term relationships between and among classes in France? Why did this occur?
2. What themes are present in the anti-Semitic piece "Anti-Semitism in Late-nineteenth-century France"? How is it characteristic of the new anti-Semitism of this era?
3. Discuss the circumstances and results of the Dreyfus Affair. What happened? What were the beliefs of the groups on each side of the controversy? Why did it divide the population of France with such antagonism?

4. What was Theodor Herzl's reaction to the Dreyfus Affair? Explain why this was such a new approach for the Jewish people. How is this related to nationalism?

5. How did Bismarck go about building a German nation after uniting its territory under a single government? What were the divisions within the new state that he felt needed control? (Make sure you include both the economic and political policies.)

6. What were the issues that challenged the British government between 1900 and the outbreak of World War I?

F. Russia

1. Examine the problems brought on by rapid industrialization in Russia. How did tsars Alexander II, Alexander III, and Nicholas II try to "solve" these problems?

2. What was meant by Russification? How was it implemented?

3. Examine the role of the Russian Populists. Who were they and what did they advocate?

4. What were the reasons behind the 1905 Russian Revolution? What was the catalyst for it? What were the results?

G. The Balkans

1. How did the treaty drawn up in 1878 in Berlin show the changing reality of the old Ottoman Empire?

2. What changes occurred in the Balkans and Turkey between the 1878 treaty and the outbreak of World War I?

H. Science and the soul

1. What impact did new scientific theories have on society?

2. Trace the development of the theory of evolution. Why was Darwin's contribution so important?

3. Read the selection under "Darwin and His Readers." What was Darwin's conclusion and what was Osterroth's reaction to it?

4. How was Darwin's theory applied to the social sciences?

5. Explain how new theories tried to explain human behavior.

6. What were Nietzsche's basic ideas?

I. Culture

1. How and why did the readership of newspapers change at the end of the nineteenth century?

2. What were the key characteristics of the modernist view in art and literature?

MULTIPLE CHOICE KEY

1. b
2. d
3. c
4. a
5. c
6. d
7. c
8. d
9. a
10. d
11. c
12. b

MATCHING KEY

1. c
2. h
3. j
4. f
5. d
6. e
7. i
8. g
9. a
10. b

TRUE/FALSE KEY

1. T
2. T
3. F
4. F
5. F
6. T
7. T
8. T
9. F
10. F

CHRONOLOGICAL ORDER KEY

4, 3, 2, 1, 5

CHAPTER 24 | The First World War

This chapter discusses the First World War. It considers what led to the war, what happened during it, and its effects on society. There were military, political, social, and economic repercussions. The consequences of the war meant that foundations of nineteenth-century economics were eroded and social upheaval ensued. In many ways, World War I opened the twentieth century.

CHAPTER OUTLINE

1. Introduction
2. The July Crisis
3. The Marne and its consequences
4. Stalemate, 1915
   a. Gallipoli and naval warfare
   b. Trench warfare
5. Slaughter in the trenches: the great battles, 1916–1917
   a. Verdun
   b. The Somme
6. War of empires
   a. Irish revolt
7. The home front
   a. Women in the war
   b. Mobilizing resources
   c. The strains of war, 1917
8. The Russian Revolution
   a. World War I and the February Revolution
   b. The Bolsheviks and the October Revolution
9. The road to German defeat, 1918
   a. The United States as a world power
   b. The peace settlement
10. Conclusion

IDENTIFY

1. Versailles Treaty
2. Brest-Litovsk
3. The July Crisis
4. Franz Ferdinand
5. Schlieffen Plan
6. Battle of the Marne
7. trench warfare
8. Gallipoli
9. Verdun
10. The Somme
11. Edmund Allenby
12. Vladimir Lenin
13. October Revolution
14. Mensheviks
15. February Revolution

MULTIPLE CHOICE

1. The spark that ignited the outbreak of war in the summer of 1914 was
   a. Russia's attack on the Ottoman Empire.
   b. the assassination of Archduke Ferdinand.
   c. Austria's attempt to annex Croatia and Macedonia.
   d. Austria's mobilization against Russia.

2. During the July Crisis
   a. Britain made a dramatic diplomatic effort to prevent the outbreak of war.
   b. Austria issued an ultimatum to Serbia.
   c. Serbia accepted all of Austria's demands.
   d. both b and c

3. Germany's Schlieffen Plan
   a. envisioned a quick German victory in France followed by a major deployment against Russia.
   b. was altered by Russian mobilization.
   c. was halted by a counteroffensive at the battle of the Marne.
   d. all of the above

4. The Allied invasion at Gallipoli
   a. was poorly planned.
   b. was the first large-scale amphibious invasion in history.
   c. was a significant defeat that cost the Allies many troops.
   d. all of the above

5. The German assault on Verdun was designed to
   a. seize this vital industrial city before moving into southern France.
   b. destroy French morale.
   c. relieve pressure from the British assault at the Somme.
   d. be a diversionary maneuver before launching another offensive to surround Paris.

6. The British responded to the Easter revolt by
   a. immediately enacting a new home rule bill that gave southern Ireland dominion status.
   b. ignoring it because the revolt had little public support in Ireland.
   c. crushing the rebellion and executing its leaders.
   d. both a and c

7. The February Revolution in Russia began when
   a. Lenin and the Bolsheviks seized power in the name of the *soviets*.
   b. women started protesting for food and political reform.
   c. the Russian military arrested the tsar.
   d. Germany demanded the overthrow of the tsar and Russia's immediate surrender.

8. Lenin and the Bolsheviks appealed to the Russian people by promising
   a. an end to the war.
   b. redistribution of land.
   c. improved working conditions.
   d. all of the above

9. The United States declared war on Germany
   a. because Germany resumed its policy of unrestricted submarine warfare.
   b. to replace the loss of Russia after the Bolshevik revolution.
   c. as a way to claim German colonies in Africa and the Pacific.
   d. to prevent a successful communist revolution in Germany.

10. The Treaty of Versailles involved a peace arrangement with _____.
    a. Turkey
    b. Austria
    c. Germany
    d. all of the above

11. In the *Economic Consequences of the Peace*, John Maynard Keynes argued that
    a. Germany should be punished so that eastern Europe could develop economically.
    b. German reparations were detrimental to a healthy world economy.
    c. German reparations were crucial to the restoration of economic prosperity to France and Britain.
    d. none of the above

12. With regard to Europe's colonies in Africa and Asia,
    a. the policy of national self-determination was essentially ignored.
    b. Europe restored Ottoman rule over Egypt and the Middle East to prevent civil war.
    c. independence was granted only to India.
    d. the League of Nations prevented Britain and France from maintaining colonial rule in both continents.

MATCHING

1. Triple Entente	a. British commander in Egypt and Palestine
2. Triple Alliance	b. a local council of soldiers and workers
3. The Somme	c. Bolshevik seizure of power
4. Edmund Allenby	d. France, Britain, Russia
5. Sinn Fein	e. promoted the Fourteen Points
6. Gavrilo Princip	f. Germany, Austria-Hungary, Italy
7. Brest-Litovsk	g. ended the war against Germany
8. *soviet*	h. 60,000 British casualties on the first day
9. Woodrow Wilson	i. shot Ferdinand
10. October Revolution	j. "Ourselves Alone"

TRUE/FALSE

1. With the outbreak of war in August 1914, most military leaders and politicians expected the war to be brief.

2. The United States declared war on Germany because of the sinking of the *Lusitania*.

3. The bloodiest battles of the war occurred in 1916 and 1917.

4. Culturally the war fostered new attitudes regarding sexuality.

5. The Allies essentially bribed Italy to join their side in war.

6. Because the Germans regarded their defensive positions as permanent, they built more elaborate trenches than either the French or the British.

7. German economic policies during the war caused inflation to increase dramatically.

8. World War I increased European involvement in the Middle East.

9. The Versailles Treaty blamed all of the great powers of Europe for the outbreak of war in 1914.

10. The United States was the leading enforcer of the League of Nations' resolutions.

PUT THE FOLLOWING ITEMS IN CHRONOLOGICAL ORDER

1. Battle of Verdun   _____

2. Assassination of Franz Ferdinand   _____

3. Battle of the Marne   _____

4. Gallipoli   _____

5. Armistice   _____

6. Treaty of Brest-Litovsk   _____

7. Bolshevik Revolution   _____

8. American declaration of war   _____

SHORT ANSWER AND ESSAY QUESTIONS

A. The July Crisis

1. What were the factors that led to World War I?
2. What were the Austro-Hungarian empire's difficulties in the Balkans? What were the reasons behind these? How would these contribute to the outbreak of the war?
3. Using the selections in *Toward World War I: Diplomacy in the Summer of 1914*, describe the perspective of Austria at the outset of the war. What is the most important point in each of these three positions?

B. The War

1. Why did the war become a stalemate?
2. What happened in the Gallipoli campaign?
3. Describe life in the trenches during World War I.
4. Why did the Allies persist with an offensive strategy?
5. What is meant by the phrase "war of attrition"?

C. War of empires

1. What role did Arabs play in the war? What did they expect in return?
2. What was the role of empires for the major states in the war?
3. Explain how events in Ireland in 1916 were linked to the war and what issues were separate from the war.

D. Home front

1. Describe the impact of the war on industry.
2. How did social norms change for women as a result of the war?
3. In the selection "One Woman's War," what do you learn about the different and often conflicting duties that women faced?
4. What would be the long-term changes for women in the workplace? Why would this happen?
5. What was the role of propaganda in the war? (Make sure you look at the illustrations in the textbook and describe them as part of your answer.)

E. The Russian Revolution

1. Explain the various problems that hampered the Russian war effort. How did these eventually lead to the overthrow of tsarist rule?
2. How did the Bolsheviks seize power? Trace the steps in the Bolshevik revolution.
3. What economic policies did the new Bolshevik government implement when it took power in 1917?

F. The road to German defeat, 1918

1. How did the Allies win the war?
2. What were the internal elements in Germany that led to its defeat?
3. What were the final stipulations in the Versailles Treaty with Germany?
4. How did desire for empire become involved in the writing of the treaties? What stipulations reflect that?

G. Overall

1. What were the changes and results of World War I?

MULTIPLE CHOICE KEY

1. b
2. b
3. d
4. d
5. b
6. c
7. b
8. d
9. a
10. c
11. b
12. a

TRUE/FALSE KEY

1. T
2. F
3. T
4. T
5. T
6. T
7. T
8. T
9. F
10. F

CHRONOLOGICAL ORDER KEY

2, 3, 4, 1, 8, 7, 6, 5

MATCHING KEY

1. d
2. f
3. h
4. a
5. j
6. i
7. g
8. b
9. e
10. c

CHAPTER 25 | Turmoil Between the Wars

This chapter deals with the period between the two world wars. It discusses the aftereffects of the First World War on governments, culture, and economy. Democracies encountered numerous domestic problems and the period also witnessed the growth of authoritarian dictatorships. The Great Depression caused immense economic and political effects. Finally, technological advances and the psychological effects of the war altered the cultural life of Europe.

CHAPTER OUTLINE

1. Introduction

2. The Soviet Union under Lenin and Stalin
   a. The Russian civil war
   b. The NEP period
   c. Stalin and the revolution from above
      i. Collectivization
      ii. The Five-Year Plans
      iii. The Great Terror

3. The emergence of fascism in Italy
   a. The rise of Mussolini

4. Weimar Germany

5. Hitler and the National Socialists
   a. Nazi Germany
      i. Nazi racism

6. The Great Depression and the democracies
   a. The origins of the Great Depression

7. Interwar culture: artists and intellectuals
   a. Interwar intellectuals
   b. Interwar artists

   c. Interwar scientific developments
   d. Mass culture and its possibilities

8. Conclusion

IDENTIFY

1. Albert Einstein
2. Leon Trotsky
3. war communism
4. New Economic Policy
5. collectivization
6. dadaists
7. The Great Terror
8. Benito Mussolini
9. T. S. Eliot
10. The Weimar constitution
11. Nazi voters
12. Heinrich Himmler
13. Nazi racial policies
14. Black Thursday
15. The New Deal

MULTIPLE CHOICE

1. The Bolsheviks triumphed in the Russian civil war because
   a. of the lack of unity among their opponents.
   b. they received support from most Russians.
   c. Trotsky's leadership created a superior communist army.
   d. all of the above

2. The New Economic Policy
   a. continued grain requisitions but allowed limited capitalism to flourish in cities.
   b. increased agricultural production by encouraging peasants to "enrich themselves."
   c. taxed the peasantry to pay for industrialization.
   d. both b and c

3. Stalin's agricultural policies
   a. continued previous policies instituted by Lenin.
   b. called for the collectivization of agriculture and elimination of the kulaks.
   c. increased agricultural production by 50 percent in his first three years.
   d. was welcomed by the majority of the peasantry, for they stood to benefit from his redistribution of land.

4. Stalin's Five Year Plans
   a. turned Russia into an industrial giant.
   b. concentrated on heavy industry and quantity over quality.
   c. created the most efficient, rationally functioning economy in Europe.
   d. both a and b

5. Mussolini achieved power in Italy
   a. by using his black-shirted militia to overthrow the king and premier.
   b. immediately following an unsuccessful communist takeover.
   c. when the king invited him to form a cabinet.
   d. none of the above

6. Which of the following statements is incorrect regarding Adolf Hitler?
   a. He was born in Austria.
   b. He served in the Austrian army in World War I.
   c. His autobiography and political manifesto is called *Mein Kampf.*
   d. His failed attempt to overthrow the government in 1923 caused him to seek power through legal means.

7. The Nazi party benefited at the polls from
   a. the continuing economic crisis.
   b. the failure of traditional parties to solve the depression.
   c. having never held power.
   d. all of the above

8. Nazi racial policy included all of the following except
   a. eugenics programs that sterilized those deemed "inferior and hereditarily tainted."
   b. pressure on Jews to convert to Christianity.
   c. the Nuremberg Decrees that stripped Jews of their citizenship.
   d. laws preventing Jews from holding public office.

9. Roosevelt's New Deal
   a. reflected the influential theories of John Maynard Keynes.
   b. increased government involvement in the economy and instituted public works programs.

   c. brought the United States out of the Great Depression.
   d. both a and b

10. Einstein's theory of relativity
    a. revolutionized the study of physics.
    b. declared space and motion to be relative to each other.
    c. included a new dimension, time.
    d. all of the above

11. Which of the following is not a characteristic shared by both Nazism and fascism?
    a. strident anticommunism
    b. a commitment to the creation of a racially pure society
    c. opposition to democracy
    d. an emphasis on nationalism over individualism

12. In Weimar Germany, the Social Democratic Party
    a. steered a moderate course to restore order and protect democracy.
    b. moved Germany closer to communism.
    c. briefly formed a governing coalition with the National Socialists.
    d. brought Germany out of the Great Depression.

MATCHING

1. Whites	a. labor camp
2. Leon Trotsky	b. Nazi propaganda leader
3. Black Tuesday	c. founded the Bauhaus
4. gulag	d. Bolshevik opponents
5. *Freikorps*	e. French coalition government
6. Joseph Goebbels	f. stock market collapse
7. Heinrich Himmler	g. night of terror against Jews
8. *Kristallnacht*	h. war commissar under Lenin
9. Popular Front	i. right-wing militias
10. Walter Gropius	j. head of the SS

TRUE/FALSE

1. The Bolsheviks' policy of war communism disrupted agricultural productivity.

2. Stalin gained power by successfully manipulating intraparty rivalries.

3. During the 1933 famine, Russia continued its agricultural exports.

4. Britain responded to the Great Depression by adopting the gold standard and taking radical measures to end unemployment.

5. The Great Terror in Russia led to a decline in literacy rates.

6. Hitler gained the admiration of urban workers by supporting labor unions and striking workers.

7. Roosevelt's New Deal solved America's unemployment problem.

8. In the Night of the Long Knives, Hitler purged the SA leadership to appease some of Germany's elites.

9. World War I exacerbated divisions between northern and southern Italy.

10. Shortly after the Reichstag fire, Hitler gained dictatorial powers.

PUT THE FOLLOWING ITEMS IN CHRONOLOGICAL ORDER

1. First Five Year Plan begins   _____

2. Death of Lenin   _____

3. Black Shirts march on Rome   _____

4. Hitler becomes chancellor   _____

5. The Great Terror   _____

SHORT ANSWER AND ESSAY QUESTIONS

A. The Soviet Union

1. In the civil war, what groups fought the Bolsheviks?
2. What was "war communism"? What were its results?
3. Trace the position and production of peasants from the end of World War I until collectivization. What were the reasons behind each of these changes?
4. How did Stalin try to bring about rapid industrialization? What were the results? Include "Stalin's Industrialization of the Soviet Union: The Tasks of Business Executives" as part of your answer.
5. What transpired during the Great Terror? What were the reasons behind it?
6. What were the results of Stalinization?

B. Italy

1. What problems existed in Italy that had been exacerbated by World War I? What additional problems arose after the war?
2. How did Mussolini gain governmental power? How did he consolidate his power?
3. Explain the three basic components of fascism.

C. Germany

1. What were the problems the Weimar government faced resulting from World War I?
2. Explain how Hitler changed his approach to gaining power after his imprisonment. Make sure you compare his previous views with the new methods.
3. How did Hitler eventually come to power? Once in power, how did he gain complete control?

4. Examine the Nazi propaganda piece by Joseph Goebbels, "Why Are We Enemies of the Jews?" to illustrate the anti-Semitic views of Nazism. Why is this propaganda?
5. What was the appeal in the *National Socialist Campaign Pamphlet, 1932*? How did it appeal to various groups?

D. The Great Depression

1. Discuss the various factors that contributed to the Great Depression.
2. Discuss how the democracies (Britain, the United States, and France) tried to mediate the circumstances caused by the depression.

E. Culture

1. What were the themes of literature after World War I?
2. In what ways did intellectuals and artists respond to World War I and the depression?
3. What was the importance of Einstein's theories?
4. In what ways did technological innovations contribute to mass culture?
5. How did authoritarian governments use mass media?

F. Overall

1. Compare the effects of the depression on the economics of Germany and the United States. Explain the political repercussions.
2. How were the ideologies of fascism and Nazism the same? How did they differ?
3. Compare and contrast the rise of the three major authoritarian dictatorships that developed between the two world wars. Explain how the dictators came to power, how they ruled, and how they maintained their power.

MULTIPLE CHOICE KEY

1. d
2. d
3. b
4. d
5. c
6. b
7. d
8. b
9. d
10. d
11. b
12. a

MATCHING KEY

1. d
2. h
3. f
4. a
5. i
6. b
7. j
8. g
9. e
10. c

TRUE/FALSE KEY

1. T
2. T
3. T
4. F
5. F
6. F
7. F
8. T
9. T
10. T

CHRONOLOGICAL ORDER KEY

3, 2, 1, 4, 5

CHAPTER 26 | The Second World War

This chapter deals with the Second World War and its implications. It begins with an examination of the reasons behind the war and the motivating forces that brought it about. It continues with descriptions of the hostilities in various theaters of the war. Within the context of the war, it explains developments on the home fronts and Hitler's policy of ethnic cleansing. Finally, it looks at the conclusion to the war.

CHAPTER OUTLINE

1. Introduction

2. The causes of the war: unsettled quarrels, economic fallout, and nationalism

3. The 1930s: challenges to the peace, appeasement, and the dishonest decade
   a. The Spanish Civil War
   b. German rearmament and the politics of appeasement

4. The outbreak of hostilities and the fall of France

5. Not alone: the Battle of Britain and the beginnings of a global war

6. The rise and ruin of nations: Germany's war in the East and the occupation of Europe

7. Racial war: ethnic cleansing and the Holocaust

8. Total war: home fronts, the war of production, bombing and the bomb
   a. The race to build the bomb
   b. Great crusades: the Allied counter attack and the dropping of the atomic bomb
      i. The Eastern Front
      ii. The Western Front
      iii. The war in the Pacific

9. Conclusion

IDENTIFY

1. appeasement
2. Spanish Civil War
3. Munich Conference
4. J. Robert Oppenheimer
5. Dunkirk
6. Stalingrad
7. Grigorii Zhukov
8. Battle of Britain
9. Winston Churchill
10. Erwin Rommel
11. Battle of the Bulge
12. Operation Barbarossa
13. *Einsatzgruppen*
14. strategic bombing
15. Hiroshima

MULTIPLE CHOICE

1. All of the following are causes of World War II identified in the text except
   a. problems resulting from attempts to redraw the boundaries of countries in eastern Europe.
   b. the inability of the League of Nations to operate effectively.
   c. the aggressive actions of the Soviet Union in promoting communist revolution abroad.
   d. the Great Depression.

2. The British policy of appeasement reflected
   a. the notion that Germany had legitimate grievances based on the Versailles Treaty.
   b. anticommunist sentiments and a desire to maintain peace.

c. the cowardice of the ruling classes.
d. both a and b

3. The League of Nations responded to the Japanese "Rape of Nanjing" by
   a. doing nothing.
   b. calling for a boycott of Japanese products imported into Europe.
   c. banning the sale of petroleum to Japan.
   d. both b and c

4. The governments of all of the following countries intervened in the Spanish Civil War except _____.
   a. the Soviet Union
   b. France
   c. Germany
   d. Italy

5. The British and French response to the German reoccupation of the Rhineland was to
   a. convene a conference in Berlin that avoided war.
   b. place economic sanctions on Germany for a period of one year.
   c. appease Hitler.
   d. both a and b

6. Among the powers not present at the Munich Conference were _____.
   a. France and Czechoslovakia
   b. Italy and the Soviet Union
   c. Czechoslovakia and the Soviet Union
   d. Italy and Czechoslovakia

7. The Battle of Britain
   a. ended when the Royal Navy prevented a German invasion.
   b. convinced Hitler to abandon plans for invading England.
   c. is considered the turning point of the war in the West.
   d. both b and c

8. Operations of the German *Einsatzgruppen*
   a. involved protecting supply lines during Operation Barbarossa.
   b. involved the mass slaughter of Jews.
   c. coordinated the resettlement of ethnic Germans in Poland.
   d. primarily centered around recruiting efforts to create a "European" fighting force to confront Bolshevism.

9. The Allied strategic bombing campaign
   a. focused exclusively on industrial and military targets.
   b. eventually destroyed Germany's will to fight.
   c. included deadly attacks against civilian populations.
   d. both b and c

10. Which of the following is incorrect regarding warfare on the Eastern Front?
    a. Soviet propaganda emphasized the struggle as a war to save the motherland.
    b. Hitler regarded the war against Russia as an ideological and racial crusade.
    c. Russians learned to exploit the weaknesses of *Blitzkrieg* tactics.
    d. Benevolent Nazi occupation policies discouraged the formation of resistance movements.

11. A "second front" was opened in Europe in June 1944
    a. when the Allies invaded Italy.
    b. with the capture of the Japanese stronghold at Okinawa.
    c. when the strategic bombing campaign was able to target German cities.
    d. with the successful invasion of Normandy.

12. Following the bombing of Nagasaki
    a. Japan surrendered unconditionally on August 14.
    b. Russia declared war on Japan.
    c. Hiroshima was hit with a second atomic bomb.
    d. both a and c

MATCHING

1. Francisco Franco
2. Neville Chamberlain
3. *Blitzkrieg*
4. wolf packs
5. Erwin Rommel
6. Operation Barbarossa
7. Charles de Gaulle
8. Auschwitz
9. Manhattan Project
10. Grigorii Zhukov

a. leader of the Free French
b. German submarine formations
c. led the Afrika Korps
d. won the Spanish Civil War
e. Russian military commander
f. American atomic bomb project
g. advocate of appeasement
h. lightning war
i. invasion of the Soviet Union
j. largest Nazi death camp

TRUE/FALSE

1. The origins of World War II can be traced back to the peace arrangements following World War I.

2. The Germans fought to the last man at Stalingrad.

3. The brutal bombing of Guernica was immortalized in a Picasso painting.

4. The Spanish Civil War convinced Hitler that Britain, France, and the Soviet Union would have difficulty establishing a united front against fascism.

5. The German conquest of Czechoslovakia convinced Britain and France to rearm rapidly.

6. The Germans rapidly defeated France by abandoning *Blitzkrieg* tactics.

7. The Vichy government went to great lengths to protect Jews in France.

8. The largest Jewish resistance movement against the Nazis was the 1943 uprising at Auschwitz.

9. Germany surrendered just before it was capable of producing an atomic weapon.

10. Japan surrendered immediately following the atomic bombing of Hiroshima.

PUT THE FOLLOWING ITEMS IN CHRONOLOGICAL ORDER

1. Japanese invasion of Manchuria   _____

2. Japanese attack at Pearl Harbor   _____

3. The Rape of Nanjing   _____

4. Italian invasion of Ethiopia   _____

5. Germany invasion of Poland   _____

6. German surrender   _____

7. Fall of France   _____

8. The Munich Conference   _____

9. Bombing of Hiroshima   _____

10. Battle of Stalingrad   _____

SHORT ANSWER AND ESSAY QUESTIONS

A. The causes of the war

1. What were the elements of the treaties ending World War I?
2. What were Japan's reasons for its expansion into Asia?

B. The 1930s: "dishonest decade"

1. Why was the Spanish Civil War regarded as a "dress rehearsal" for World War II?
2. What was the policy of "appeasement"?
3. What steps did Hitler take to expand its territory and military power?
4. Examine the chronology chart "The Road to World War II, 1931–1940," up to the invasion of Poland, and explain how each of these steps contributed to the outbreak of the war.

C. The outbreak of hostilities

1. Why did Poland fall so quickly?
2. Why was the Eastern Front a new kind of war?

D. Global war

1. What were the reasons behind the continued British resistance to Germany in 1940 while they fought alone against them?
2. What were Winston Churchill's gifts? How did these contribute to the survival and success of Britain?
3. What regions were involved which made this a global war? How did each of these become involved?
4. In the Pacific, why did the Japanese strategy depend on destroying the American Pacific Fleet simultaneously with their assaults on the Philippines, Dutch East Indies, and Southwest Asia?

E. Continental theater

1. What was Hitler's concept of German national destiny? How did this affect his military policy?
2. Why did Hitler choose to annex certain conquests to Germany but settled for occupation in others?
3. What kind of resistance existed in occupied countries?
4. Explain the difference between collaboration, resistance, and self-interested indifference. How did people decide where they stood?

F. Ethnic cleansing

1. What were the various groups that Hitler's forces attacked and tried to eliminate? What were the reactions of other states?
2. Why was it so difficult to oppose the Nazi policies of ethnic cleansing?
3. What was the method of execution in the selection on *The Holocaust* reading "The Death Camps"?
4. How does "Himmler's Instructions to the SS" explain why the extermination of the Jews was considered the right policy?

G. The home fronts

1. How and why were the Allies able to have such high industrial production for the war? Why was this so important?
2. How did the war transform the home fronts?

H. The fronts

1. What were the fronts in Europe? How did each of these develop?
2. Examine the chronology chart on "The Western Front" and explain what made each of these so important.
3. What countries were involved in the war in the Pacific? How did the war unfold there?

I. Overall

1. Write an essay examining the depression and how it contributed to the war. Include the depression's effects on various states and on the outbreak of the war. You may also include some of the information on the depression found in Chapter 25.

2. Explain the course of the war in all theaters of operations (Africa, Europe, the Pacific, the Atlantic, and Asia).
3. Why was this war so murderous?

MULTIPLE CHOICE KEY

1. c
2. d
3. a
4. b
5. c
6. c
7. b
8. b
9. c
10. d
11. d
12. a

MATCHING KEY

1. d
2. g
3. h
4. b
5. c
6. i
7. a
8. j
9. f
10. e

TRUE/FALSE KEY

1. T
2. F
3. T
4. T
5. T
6. F
7. F
8. F
9. F
10. F

CHRONOLOGICAL ORDER KEY

1, 4, 3, 8, 5, 7, 2, 10, 6, 9

CHAPTER 27

The Cold War World: Global Politics, Economic Recovery, and Cultural Change

This chapter discusses the changes brought to the world by the Second World War. The end of the war brought the Cold War, which centralized politics, culture, and economics around twin poles of superpowers. There was also decentralizing around the globe as old empires broke apart and new nations emerged. All of these factors contributed to a new cultural view of the world.

CHAPTER OUTLINE

1. Introduction
2. The cold war and a divided continent
   a. The Iron Curtain
   b. The Marshall Plan
   c. Two worlds and the race for the Bomb
   d. Khrushchev and the "Thaw"
3. Economic Renaissance
   a. Repression in Eastern Europe
   b. European economic integration
      i. Economic development in the East
      ii. The Welfare State
      iii. European politics
4. Revolution, Anti-Colonialism, and the Cold War
   a. The Chinese Revolution
      i. The Korean War
   b. Decolonization
      i. The British empire unravels
         (1) Palestine
         (2) Africa
         (3) Crisis in Suez and the end of an era
      ii. French decolonization
         (1) The first Vietnam War, 1946–1954
         (2) Algeria

5. Postwar culture and thought
   a. The black presence
   b. Existentialism
   c. Memory and amnesia: the aftermath of war

6. Conclusion

IDENTIFY

1. cold war
2. Iron Curtain
3. Marshall Plan
4. NATO
5. Warsaw Pact
6. Nikita Khrushchev
7. Comecon
8. Charles de Gaulle
9. Korean War
10. Mohandas Gandhi
11. apartheid
12. Ho Chi Minh
13. FLN
14. existentialism
15. Treaty of Rome

MULTIPLE CHOICE

1. The general pattern of political development in Eastern Europe following World War II included all of the following except
   a. the establishment of coalition governments excluding former Nazi sympathizers.
   b. the creation of parliamentary democracies following free elections.

c. the creation of coalition governments dominated by communists.

d. the establishment of a one-party state.

2. The famous "Iron Curtain" speech was delivered in Missouri by _____.
   a. Franklin Roosevelt
   b. Harry Truman
   c. Winston Churchill
   d. George Marshall

3. The Soviets cut off access to Berlin after the Western Allies
   a. intervened in the Greek Civil War on behalf of the monarchy.
   b. organized NATO and began preparations for German rearmament.
   c. began to create a single government for their German territories.
   d. protested Soviet violations of the agreements at Yalta and Potsdam.

4. According to the Truman Doctrine
   a. the United States intended to roll back the gains communism made in Eastern Europe through direct military intervention.
   b. the United States agreed to airlift supplies to West Berlin.
   c. the United States called for the reunification of Germany.
   d. none of the above

5. The Soviet response to the Marshall Plan and NATO
   a. was to establish its own military alliances.
   b. was ineffectual and largely centered around denunciations of America during meetings of the United Nations.
   c. allowed increased economic and political reforms in Eastern Europe.
   d. both b and c

6. In the "secret speech" of 1956
   a. Stalin warned Eastern Europe not to accept Marshall Plan assistance.
   b. Khrushchev denounced the harshness of the Stalin years.
   c. Khrushchev adopted a policy of "peaceful coexistence" with the West.
   d. Russia announced that the Iron Curtain accurately described the political arrangement in Eastern Europe.

7. In 1961, the East German government responded to the exodus of its citizens to the West by
   a. imprisoning for life family members of those who left.
   b. building a wall between the two sectors of Berlin.
   c. building a wall dividing East Germany from West Germany.
   d. all of the above

8. During the Korean War, MacArthur
   a. was relieved of his command.
   b. launched an amazing amphibious assault behind North Korean lines.
   c. wanted to reverse the Chinese Revolution.
   d. all of the above

9. Apartheid was a system that
   a. segregated black South Africans into "homelands."
   b. allowed for the deliberate withdrawal of British authority in Rhodesia.
   c. was the term used to describe decolonization.
   d. none of the above

10. The crisis in Suez
    a. strengthened France's rule in Algeria.
    b. strengthened the natural alliance between America and Britain.
    c. ended Britain's role as a significant imperial power in the Middle East.
    d. forced Nasser from power.

11. According to the 1954 Geneva Accords
    a. India was partitioned to create the country of Pakistan.
    b. Vietnam was divided into two states.
    c. the Dutch withdrew from Indonesia.
    d. the United States pledged to support French colonial rule in Indochina.

12. All of the following are results of the Algerian war except
    a. independence for Algeria.
    b. the immigration to France of hundreds of thousands of Algerians.
    c. the collapse of de Gaulle's government.
    d. the reevaluation within France of its role as a modern power.

MATCHING

1. Eastern bloc
2. Marshall Plan
3. Comecon
4. Warsaw Pact
5. Kennan
6. Solzhenitsyn
7. Jiang Jeishi
8. FLN
9. de Beauvoir
10. Arendt

a. Soviet military alliance
b. author of *Origins of Totalitarianism*
c. Poland, Hungary, Romania, Bulgaria
d. author of *The Second Sex*
e. economic aid to Western Europe
f. fought the French in Algeria
g. Chinese Nationalist leader
h. promoted the policy of containment
i. described life in the Gulag Archipelago
j. Soviet version of the Marshall Plan

TRUE/FALSE

1. The Bretton Woods agreements provided a framework for reducing nuclear weapons in Europe.

2. Following World War II, the Allies divided Germany into three occupation zones.

3. NATO members recognized that an attack on one of them meant, in effect, an attack on all.

4. Unlike Stalin, Khrushchev traveled widely.

5. In the 1950s, the Soviet military crushed opposition movements in Hungary and Poland.

6. The European Economic Community sought to abolish trade barriers and to allow for the free movement of labor and capital among its members.

7. Charles de Gaulle withdrew French forces from NATO and cultivated better relations with the Soviet Union.

8. Shortly after Israel announced its independence, it was invaded by five neighboring states.

9. Great Britain was an original member of the Common Market.

10. Historians now conclude that Marshall Plan funds alone fueled Western Europe's economic miracle.

PUT THE FOLLOWING ITEMS IN CHRONOLOGICAL ORDER

1. Formation of the Warsaw Pact   _____

2. Berlin wall built   _____

3. Creation of Israel   _____

4. Treaty of Rome   _____

5. Berlin Airlift   _____

SHORT ANSWER AND ESSAY QUESTIONS

A. Cold war and divided continent

1. What were the major changes in the balance of power after the war?
2. Define the cold war and explain its causes.
3. Why did Winston Churchill argue, in his Iron Curtain speech, that the old doctrine of a balance of power was unsound? What was Khrushchev's view of capitalism as stated in his "Report to the Communist Party Congress"? (Under the documents *The Cold War: Soviet and American Views*)
4. What was the goal of the Marshall Plan? Describe how it functioned.
5. What changes did Khrushchev bring to the USSR?
6. How did the literature of Soviet writers reflect the political status of the USSR?
7. What transpired in Eastern European states after Stalin's death?

B. Economic renaissance

1. Explain the various factors involved in Western Europe's economic recovery.
2. How did governmental policies in Western Europe contribute to economic growth, particularly in West Germany?
3. Trace the way in which international organizations brought Western Europeans together economically.
4. What was the new concept regarding social welfare?

C. Revolution, anticolonialism, and the cold war

1. Trace the stages and developments of the Chinese Revolution. Discuss its importance.
2. Explain what led to the Korean War and how this was part of the worldwide divisions between East and West.
3. Explain the processes of decolonization, giving examples of three ways in which it was carried out.
4. Explain how various understandings and promises were in conflict in the establishment of Palestine and Israel.
5. Write an essay describing the decolonization process in India.
6. Explain Gandhi's reasoning, in the document "Mohandas Gandhi and Nonviolent Anticolonialism," that the nonviolent approach to colonialism would work?
7. What was the process of decolonization in Western African colonies?
8. What made the decolonization process different in South Africa, Rhodesia, and Egypt?
9. What made France's decolonization process so much bloodier in Vietnam and Algeria? How did this change the domestic politics in France?
10. Why does Fannon, in the selection "Anticolonialism and Violence," believe violence would be part of the decolonization process?
11. What divisions were there among the population in Algeria? How did these make the situation more complex?

D. Postwar culture and thought

1. What themes defined the postwar culture?
2. What were the themes of existentialism? How were some a reaction to the war? What kinds of questions were being pursued?

E. Overall

1. Compare the post–World War II economies in Eastern and Western Europe.
2. Explain the links between decolonization, World War II, and the cold war.

MULTIPLE CHOICE KEY

1. b
2. c
3. c
4. d
5. a
6. b
7. b
8. d
9. a
10. c
11. b
12. c

MATCHING KEY

1. c
2. e
3. j
4. a
5. h
6. i
7. g
8. f
9. d
10. b

TRUE/FALSE KEY

1. F
2. F
3. T
4. T
5. F
6. T
7. T
8. T
9. F
10. F

CHRONOLOGICAL ORDER KEY

3, 5, 1, 4, 2

CHAPTER 28

Red Flags and Velvet Revolutions: The End of the Cold War, 1960–1990

This chapter describes the political changes that ultimately led to the end of the cold war. Beginning in the 1960s, a number of social and economic issues came to the fore, which led to an eventual transformation of outlook. It was a time of a new awareness of problems for various social groups. In the late 1960s tensions exploded on a number of fronts. The mid-1970s brought economic crises in both the East and the West. The collapse of the Eastern bloc and the disintegration of the Soviet Union transformed the political outlook of the world.

CHAPTER OUTLINE

1. Introduction

2. Society and class: 1945–1968
   a. Art and painting
   b. Film
      i. Hollywood and the Americanization of culture
   c. Gender roles and sexual revolution

3. Social movements during the 1960s
   a. The civil rights movement
   b. The antiwar movement
   c. The student movement
      i. 1968
      ii. Paris
      iii. Prague

4. Economic stagnation: the price of success
   a. Solidarity in Poland

5. Europe recast: the collapse of communism and the end of the Soviet Union
   a. Gorbachev and Soviet reform
   b. Fall of the Berlin Wall
   c. The collapse of the Soviet Union
   d. Post-revolutionary troubles: Eastern Europe after 1989

6. Conclusion

IDENTIFY

1. rock and roll
2. abstract expressionism
3. Americanization of Western culture
4. sexual revolution
5. Betty Friedan
6. Martin Luther King, Jr.
7. Antiwar Movement
8. The Student Movement
9. Prague spring
10. Leonid Brezhnev
11. Solidarity
12. Mikhail Gorbachev
13. Boris Yeltsin
14. Velvet Revolutions
15. Slobodan Milosevic

MULTIPLE CHOICE

1. All of the following represent significant postwar developments in Western Europe except
   a. a drastic decline in labor union power.
   b. the percentage of government employees increased.
   c. secondary education became compulsory.
   d. the number of foreign laborers increased.

2. The center of modern art world is _____.
   a. Paris
   b. London
   c. New York
   d. Berlin

3. The dominance of Hollywood and the rise of the American film industry benefited from
   a. the huge domestic audience in America.
   b. the devastation caused by World War II.
   c. the lack of qualified European movie directors.
   d. both a and b

4. The sexual revolution involved all of the following except
   a. more women in the workforce.
   b. the increasing sexual nature of mass consumer culture.
   c. a dramatic increase in the birthrate in the 1970s and 1980s.
   d. the legalization of contraception throughout the West.

5. In *The Feminine Mystique*, Friedan
   a. exposed the cultural contradictions of modern feminism for endorsing abortion as a means of birth control.
   b. revealed how the combined efforts of the media, the social sciences and advertising lowered women's expectations and possibilities.
   c. published the names of 343 prominent women who had abortions to promote widespread availability of birth control.
   d. both a and c

6. America's involvement in the Vietnam War
   a. resulted in the reelection of Lyndon Johnson.
   b. magnified the country's racial inequality according to Martin Luther King, Jr.
   c. escalated under President Kennedy, who ordered the strategic bombing of North Vietnam.
   d. both a and b

7. Student protests in France
   a. centered on demands that universities be modernized.
   b. prompted sympathy strikes by French workers.
   c. brought down de Gaulle's presidency.
   d. both a and b

8. All of the following events occurred in 1968 except
   a. the assassination of Martin Luther King, Jr.
   b. the end of de Gaulle's government.
   c. student protests in Paris.
   d. the Prague spring.

9. Brezhnev responded to government reforms in Czechoslovakia
   a. by ignoring the situation and letting conservative Czechoslovakians restore order.
   b. with military intervention.

   c. by instituting martial law and conducting a bloody purge of Communist parties throughout Eastern Europe, reminiscent of Stalin.
   d. none of the above

10. Margaret Thatcher rose to power in England by championing
    a. the expansion of the welfare state.
    b. a greater role for government in directing the economy.
    c. lower taxes, privatization, and reduced trade union power.
    d. all of the above

11. Mikhail Gorbachev's policy of perestroika
    a. involved a restructuring of the Russian economy.
    b. called for competitive elections and term limits on office holders.
    c. favored the creation of a mixed economy.
    d. all of the above

12. The bloodiest revolution to end communist rule occurred in which East European country?
    a. Rumania
    b. Hungary
    c. East Germany
    d. Czechoslovakia

MATCHING

1. "race music"
2. Jackson Pollock
3. Andy Warhol
4. Kinsey reports
5. Alexander Dubček
6. Malcolm X
7. glasnost
8. Mikhail Gorbachev
9. Slobodan Milosevic
10. Chechnya

a. black nationalist
b. described American sexual behavior
c. site of a bloody separatist war against Russia
d. revoked the Brezhnev Doctrine
e. rock and roll
f. Serbian nationalist
g. abstract expressionist
h. pop artist
i. intellectual openness
j. promoted socialism with a human face

TRUE/FALSE

1. The expansion of the welfare state rendered trade unions unnecessary.

2. In 1991, the European Union created a single currency which was used throughout Western Europe.

3. Martin Luther King, Jr. embraced the philosophy of nonviolence promoted by Gandhi.

4. Jaruzelski led the solidarity movement in Poland.

5. Unlike in Western Europe, the economies of Eastern Europe continued to grow in the 1970s and early 1980s.

6. The Soviet Union used the Brezhnev Doctrine to justify military intervention in Eastern Europe.

7. Boris Yeltsin helped prevent the overthrow of Gorbachev's government by hard-line communists.

8. Increased antiwar demonstrations and student protests occurred in the wake of the Tet Offensive.

9. Serbians in Bosnia and Kosovo carried out a policy of ethnic cleansing.

10. Roman Catholicism, Eastern Orthodoxy, and Lutheranism are three dominant religious influences and sources of division in the Balkans.

PUT THE FOLLOWING ITEMS IN CHRONOLOGICAL ORDER

1. OPEC oil embargo   _____

2. Velvet Revolutions   _____

3. End of Milosovic's rule   _____

4. Prague spring   _____

5. End of the USSR   _____

SHORT ANSWER AND ESSAY QUESTIONS

A. Society, class, and culture: 1945–1968

1. Discuss the ways in which daily life was transformed between 1945 and 1968.
2. Discuss how values and lives were transformed by changes in mass consumption.
3. Explain how the mass culture of a "new generation" affected all of society.
4. Examine the role of music worldwide in the "new generation."
5. Explain the various types and styles of art in the postwar era. How were these part of a "postwar" culture?
6. What were the themes in film and literature in the late 1940s and 1950s? Give examples of how these themes were conveyed. How did the films from different countries reflect different themes of the new culture?
7. How and why was there a new view toward sexuality?
8. How do the selections from "The Woman Question on Both Sides of the Atlantic" show a new awareness of society's definition of femininity?
9. What spurred the social movements of the 1960s?

10. Discuss the reasons behind student unrest throughout the world in the 1960s.
11. Use the selection "Ludvik Vaculik, Two Thousand Words" to help explain the motivation behind the Prague spring.
12. Describe the events of the Prague spring and explain its importance.

B. Economics

1. What caused the economic stagnation of the 1970s and 1980s?
2. Trace the changes to the economy in the 1970s and 1980s.

C. Europe recast

1. Explain how Gorbachev brought changes to the Soviet Union.
2. What problems did the Soviet Union face within its sphere of influence?
3. Trace the changes in the politics of Eastern European states. How were these political changes connected to each other and what was unique for each state?
4. What happened in the Soviet Union that brought changes to the government? Why did this occur?
5. How did the Eastern European states adapt to the changes after the fall of the Berlin wall and the end of the Soviet Union?
6. Why did the Balkans again become a center of conflict?

D. Overall

1. Explain how and why the youth of the "Sixties" were such a potent force.
2. How did internal questions of ethnic and religious differences affect the various countries?

MULTIPLE CHOICE KEY

1. a
2. c
3. d
4. c
5. b
6. b
7. d
8. b
9. b
10. c
11. d
12. a

MATCHING KEY	TRUE/FALSE KEY
1. e	1. F
2. g	2. F
3. h	3. T
4. b	4. F
5. j	5. F
6. a	6. T
7. i	7. T
8. d	8. T
9. f	9. T
10. c	10. F

CHRONOLOGICAL ORDER KEY

4, 1, 2, 5, 3

CHAPTER 29

A World without Walls: Globalization and the West

This chapter examines where we are now and assesses current trends throughout the world. The first of these trends concerns the interconnectedness of the world through what is called "globalization." The chapter also looks at "postcolonial" politics and the experiences of former colonies. The final section of the chapter focuses on the complexity and importance of Middle Eastern politics and its effects on the rest of the world, particularly in the West.

CHAPTER OUTLINE

1. Introduction

2. Liquid modernity? The flow of money, ideas, and peoples
   a. Demographics of global health

3. After empire: Postcolonial politics in the global era
   a. Emancipation and ethnic conflict in Africa
   b. Economic power on the Pacific rim

4. A new center of gravity: Israel, oil, and political Islam in the Middle East
   a. The Arab-Israeli conflict
   b. Oil, power, and economics
   c. The rise of political Islam
      i. Iran's Islamic revolution
   d. Iran, Iraq, and unintended consequences of the cold war

5. Violence beyond bounds: War and terrorism in the twenty-first century

6. Conclusion

IDENTIFY

1. globalization
2. neoliberalism
3. DNA
4. Nelson Mandela
5. Hutus
6. Africa's world war
7. the "Tigers"
8. *intifada*
9. OPEC
10. Sayyid Qutb
11. Reza Pahlavi
12. Ayatollah Khomeini
13. Saddam Hussein
14. *mujahidin*
15. al Qaeda

MULTIPLE CHOICE

1. The development of political, social, economic, and cultural networks around the world is called _____.
   a. internationalization
   b. globalization
   c. the Internet
   d. outsourcing

2. Which of the following is an example of globalization?
   a. the Internet
   b. the free flow of labor
   c. outsourcing of jobs
   d. all of the above

3. An example of the globalization of judicial power is the
   _____.
   a. United States Supreme Court
   b. the International Monetary Fund
   c. the International Criminal Court
   d. the World Bank

4. When the United States abandoned the gold standard,
   a. formal regulations on currencies, international banking, and lending disappeared.
   b. the world economy became tied to the English pound.
   c. the International Monetary Fund declared bankruptcy and faded away shortly thereafter.
   d. all of the above

5. Among the most profitable commodities sold in the West and produced in poor, postcolonial regions are _____.
   a. steel products
   b. software programs
   c. drugs
   d. automobiles

6. The demographic crisis facing Western Europe involves
   a. a declining birthrate coupled with longer life spans.
   b. an expanding birthrate but declining life spans.
   c. an excessive concentration of its population in urban areas.
   d. none of the above

7. The system known as *apartheid* refers to
   a. the bloody civil wars and corrupt tyrannies following the withdrawal of colonial powers from Africa.
   b. the brutal system of racial oppression in South Africa.
   c. the ethnic civil wars in Benin and Mozambique in the early 1990s.
   d. a new form of social democracy that guaranteed both political and economic equality.

8. In the 1990s, Rwanda was home to
   a. a series of wars observers have called "Africa's world war."
   b. an industrial movement that served as an economic model for Western Africa.
   c. a nonviolent handing over of power after years of rule by a minority white population.
   d. a well-orchestrated genocidal campaign.

9. Which of the following correctly reflects the views of Sayyid Qutb?
   a. Western influence has had a detrimental effect on the Islamic world.
   b. To energize the Arab world, Islam needs to modernize.
   c. Postcolonial Arab political elites have abandoned true Islam.
   d. both a and c

10. All of the following characterized the Iranian government under the shah except
    a. the extension of democracy.
    b. support for the West during the cold war.
    c. repression conducted by the army and secret police.
    d. acceptance of some Western cultural ideas.

11. A coalition of Western and Arab powers went to war with Iraq because Iraq
    a. invaded Iran and threatened to use chemical weapons.
    b. under Saddam Hussein had a deplorable human rights record.
    c. invaded Kuwait.
    d. provided a base for al Qaeda to train recruits and a permanent home for its leaders.

12. All of the following are accurate regarding al Qaeda except
    a. its official leader was Osama bin Laden.
    b. it grew out of the *mujahidin* movement in Afghanistan.
    c. its actions have been against only American and European interests outside of the Islamic world.
    d. its attack on September 11 prompted America to go to war in Afghanistan.

MATCHING

1. globalization
2. neoliberals
3. Rupert Murdoch
4. human genome
5. Nelson Mandela
6. The "Tigers"
7. *intifada*
8. Reza Pahlavi
9. Ayatollah Khomeini
10. *mujahidin*

a. all chromosomes and genes found in DNA
b. Palestinian uprising against Israel
c. fought the Soviets in Afghanistan
d. integration
e. stress the value of free markets
f. ruled Iran after the shah
g. U.S.-backed shah of Iran
h. media mogul
i. led the African National Congress
j. Pacific rim states

TRUE/FALSE

1. Globalization is an entirely new phenomenon.

2. One of the benefits of globalization is its acceptance around the world as a way to preserve one's native culture.

3. The United States, France, and the Soviet Union supported Iraq in its war against Iran.

4. As a result of globalization, the world's economies have become more integrated.

5. The Middle East oil boom has eroded economic inequality throughout the region.

6. For the Pacific Rim countries, the greatest period of economic expansion occurred in the 1990s.

7. Implicit in the term *postcolonial* is an understanding that even with independence, the legacies of colonialism survived.

8. President Ronald Reagan helped broker a peace agreement between Israel and Egypt.

9. Militant political Islam gained strength as Pan-Arab nationalism declined.

10. Following the fall of the shah, Iran based its legal system on Islamic law.

PUT THE FOLLOWING ITEMS IN CHRONOLOGICAL ORDER

1. Khomeini takes power in Iran   _____

2. Formation of OPEC   _____

3. Egypt and Israel sign peace agreement   _____

4. First *intifada* erupts   _____

5. Iraq invades Kuwait   _____

SHORT ANSWER AND ESSAY QUESTIONS

A. Globalization

1. What are the features of globalization?
2. How has globalization changed economic perceptions?
3. What are the effects of globalization on everyday life?
4. Examine the impact of the flow of information on people's lives.
5. How does the flow of information affect political struggles and discussions?
6. In what areas was there a large growth in population? What contributed to this growth in population?
7. How has health been affected by changes in globalization of societies?
8. Explain the demographic problems and the reasons behind these problems faced by the Western states.
9. What medical changes have been produced by research during the final years of the twentieth century and the beginning of the twenty-first? Explain their influence on society.

B. After empire

1. Trace the development of South Africa's governmental changes. How is this development an example of one of the major trends in the newly decolonized world?
2. How were ethnic conflicts unleashed in the decolonized world?
3. Discuss the rise of East Asia as an economic power.

C. Middle East

1. How did the global demand for oil reshape the politics, religion, and society in the Middle East?
2. What problems did the Palestinians face which contributed to the *intifada*?
3. Explain why oil is such a crucial factor and strategic component to the politics of the Middle East.
4. What are the characteristics of political Islam? Trace its development and rise in the Middle East.
5. How did the government of Iran change during the 1970s? What were the reasons behind these changes and the results?
6. How were the residues of the cold war manifested in the states of the Middle East?

D. Violence beyond bounds

1. What are the characteristics of terrorist organizations?
2. Has globalization changed the politics of terrorism?

MULTIPLE CHOICE KEY

1. b
2. d
3. c
4. a
5. c
6. a
7. b
8. d
9. d
10. a
11. c
12. c

MATCHING KEY

1. d
2. e
3. h
4. a
5. i
6. j
7. b
8. g
9. f
10. c

TRUE/FALSE KEY

1. F
2. F
3. T
4. T
5. T
6. F
7. T
8. F
9. T
10. T

CHRONOLOGICAL ORDER KEY

2, 3, 1, 4, 5